RESUMES
FOR
PERFORMING
ARTS
CAREERS

VGM Professional Resumes Series

RESUMES FOR PERFORMING ARTS CAREERS

The Editors of VGM Career Horizons

Printed on recyclable paper

VGM Career Horizons
NTC/Contemporary Publishing Company
Lincolnwood, Illinois USA

ACKNOWLEDGMENT

We would like to acknowledge the assistance of Dorothy Morris
in compiling and editing this book.

Library of Congress Cataloging-in Publication Data

Resumes for performing arts careers / the editors of VGM Career Horizons.

    p.   cm. — (VGM professional resumes series)
  ISBN 0-8442-4521-6 (alk. paper)
    1. Performing arts—Vocational guidance—United States.
2. Résumés (Employment) I. VGM Career Horizons (Firm) II. Series.
PN1580.R47 1997
791'.02373—dc21   96-37069
                                                CIP

CONTENTS

Introduction

Your resume is your first impression on a prospective employer. Though you may be articulate, intelligent, and charming in person, a poor resume may prevent you from ever having the opportunity to demonstrate your interpersonal skills, because a poor resume may prevent you from ever being called for an interview. While few people have ever been hired solely on the basis of their resume, a well-written, well-organized resume can go a long way toward helping you land an interview, audition, or job. Your resume's main purpose is to get you that opportunity. The rest is up to you and the employer. If you both feel that you are right for the job and the job is right for you, chances are you will be hired.

A resume must catch the reader's attention yet still be easy to read and to the point. Resume styles have changed over the years. Today, brief and focused resumes are preferred. No longer do employers have the patience, or the time, to review several pages of solid type. A resume should be only one page long, if possible, and never more than two pages. Time is a precious commodity in today's business world and the resume that is concise and straightforward will usually be the one that gets noticed

Let's not make the mistake, though, of assuming that writing a brief resume means that you can take less care in preparing it. A successful resume takes time and thought, and if you are willing to make the effort, the rewards are well worth it. Think of your resume as a sales tool with the product being you. You want to sell yourself to a prospective employer. This book is designed to help you prepare a resume that will help you further your career—to land that next job, or first job, or to return to the work force after years of absence. So, read on. Make the effort and reap the rewards that a strong resume can being to your career. Let's get to it!

Chapter One

THE ELEMENTS OF A GOOD RESUME

A winning performing arts resume is made of the elements that employers are most interested in seeing when reviewing a job applicant. These basic elements are the essential ingredients of a successful resume and become the actual sections of your resume. The following is a list of elements that may be used in a resume. Some are essential; some are optional. We will be discussing these in this chapter in order to give you a better understanding of each element's role in the makeup of your resume:

1. Heading
2. Objective
3. Statistics/Personal Information
4. Work Experience
5. Education
6. Honors
7. Training
8. Certificates and Licenses
9. Professional Memberships and Affiliations
10. Special Skills
11. References

The first step in preparing your resume is to gather together information about yourself and your past accomplishments. Later you will refine this information, rewrite it in the most effective language, and organize it into the most attractive layout. First, let's take a look at each of these important elements individually.

Heading

The heading may seem to be a simple enough element in your resume, but be careful not to take it lightly. The heading should be placed at the top of your resume and should include your name, instrument (if applicable), home address, and telephone numbers. If you can take calls at your current place of business, include your business number. If this is not possible, or if you can afford it, purchase an answering machine that allows you to retrieve your messages while you are away from home. This way you can make sure you don't miss important phone calls. Always include your phone number on your resume. It is crucial that when prospective employers need to have immediate contact with you, they can.

Statistics/Personal Information

For many performance occupations, especially when a photo is required for application, personal statistics are desired. For singers and actors, height, weight, hair color and eye color are standard information. Include your date of birth at your discretion; this information is most relevant for performers just starting out. If you are not comfortable stating your date of birth, you can indicate an age range that you feel is realistic given your experience and appearance.

Objective

A job objective helps employers know the direction that you see yourself heading, so that they can determine whether your goals are in line with the position available. The objective is normally one sentence long and describes your employment goals clearly and concisely.

In most cases, this element is not necessary. The objective statement is better left out if you are uncertain of the exact title of the job you seek. In such a case, the inclusion of an overly specific objective statement could result in your not being considered for a variety of acceptable positions; you should be sure to incorporate this information in your cover letter, instead.

In general, objectives are only stated on performing arts resumes when the applicant is seeking a teaching or management position.

Work Experience

This element is arguably the most important of them all. It will provide the central focus of your resume, so it is necessary that this section be as complete as possible. Only by examining your work experience in depth can you get to the heart of your accomplishments and present them in a way that demonstrates the strength of your qualifications. Of course, someone just out of school will have less work experience than someone who has been working for a number of years, but the amount of information isn't the most important thing—rather, how it is presented and how it highlights you as a person and as a worker will be what counts.

As you work on this section of your resume, be aware of the need for accuracy. You'll want to include all necessary information about each of your jobs, which may include role or position; dates; company; city and state; related awards, honors, or scholarships; and accomplishments such as special skills related to the job. If you haven't received any special awards, that's all right—this area may not be relevant to certain jobs.

The most common way to list your work experience is in *reverse chronological order* within each category. In other words, start with your most recent job and work your way backwards. This way your prospective employer sees your current (and often most important) job before seeing your past jobs. Your most recent position, if the most important, should also be the one that includes the most information, as compared to your previous positions. If you are just out of school, show your summer employment and part-time work, though in this case your education will most likely be more important than your work experience. The order of each category may vary, and will be discussed in Chapter 3.

The following worksheets will help you gather information about your past jobs.

WORK EXPERIENCE
Job One:

Role/Position _____

Dates (Year) _____

Employer (Opera, Theater Company, Orchestra) _____

City, State _____

Major Details (Name of show, opera, or orchestral piece; status of position: principal oboe, understudy,

title role, etc.) _____

_____

_____

_____

_____

_____

_____

_____

_____

_____

_____

_____

Related Skills, Honors, and Accomplishments _____

_____

_____

_____

_____

_____

_____

Job Two:

Role/Position _____

Dates _____

Employer _____

City, State _____

Major Details _____

_____

_____

_____

_____

_____

_____

_____

_____

_____

_____

_____

Related Skills, Honors, and Accomplishments_____

_____

_____

_____

_____

_____

_____

Job Three:

Role/Position _____

Dates _____

Employer _____

City, State _____

Major Details _____

_____

_____

_____

_____

_____

_____

_____

_____

_____

_____

Related Skills, Honors, and Accomplishments _____

_____

_____

_____

_____

_____

_____

_____

Job Four:

Role/Position _____

Dates _____

Employer _____

City, State _____

Major Details _____

_____

_____

_____

_____

_____

_____

_____

_____

_____

_____

_____

Related Skills, Honors, and Accomplishments _____

_____

_____

_____

_____

_____

_____

_____

Education

Education should appear at or near the bottom of a performance resume. The reason for this is that a prospective employer is primarily interested in your field experience, honors, and specific hands-on training, including names of teachers (who may be known to the employer). This information is of more immediate interest to a prospective employer than the name of your college and the degree conferred; however, academic experience is also important and should not be left off your resume. You will want to be sure to include any degrees or certificates you received, your major area of concentration, any honors, and any relevant activities. Again, be sure to list your most recent schooling first. If you have completed graduate-level work, begin with that and work in reverse chronological order through your undergraduate education. If you have completed an undergraduate degree, you may choose whether to list your high school experience or not. This should be done only if your high school grade-point average was well above average.

The following worksheets will help you gather information for this section of your resume. Also included are supplemental worksheets for honors and for activities. Sometimes honors and activities are listed in a section separate from education, most often near the end of the resume.

EDUCATION

School _____

Major or Area of Concentration _____

Degree _____

Date _____

School _____

Major or Area of Concentration _____

Degree _____

Date _____

Honors

Here, you should list any awards, honors, or memberships in honorary societies that you have received. Usually these are of an academic nature, (scholarships, stipends, etc.), but they can also be for special achievement in sports, clubs, or other school activities. Always be sure to include the name of the organization honoring you and the date(s) received. Use the worksheet below to help gather your honors information.

HONORS

Honor _____

Awarding Organization _____

Date(s) _____

Honor _____

Awarding Organization _____

Date(s) _____

Honor _____

Awarding Organization _____

Date(s) _____

Honor _____

Awarding Organization _____

Date(s) _____

Training

Your educational background will often consist of elements more specific than the name of your school(s) and the year you graduated. Additional training may consist of names of teachers, coaches, or conductors. In this section, add any skills you may have acquired that require special explanation, such as years of study.

Sometimes you will see this information included in the Special Skills area, discussed later in this chapter.

TRAINING

Area of Study/Skill Acquired _____

Teachers, Coaches, etc. _____

_____

Location _____

Area of Study/Skill Acquired _____

Teachers, Coaches, etc. _____

_____

Location _____

Area of Study/Skill Acquired _____

Teachers, Coaches, etc. _____

_____

Location _____

Area of Study/Skill Acquired _____

Teachers, Coaches, etc. _____

_____

Location _____

As your work experience increases through the years, your school activities and honors will play less of a role in your resume, and eventually you will most likely only list your degree and any major honors you received. This is due to the fact that, as time goes by, your job performance becomes the most important element in your resume. Through time, your resume should change to reflect this.

Certificates and Licenses

The next potential element of your resume is certificates and licenses. You should list these if the job you are seeking requires them and you, of course, have acquired them. If you have applied for a license, but have not yet received it, use the phrase "application pending."

License requirements vary by state. If you have moved or you are planning to move to another state, be sure to check with the appropriate board or licensing agency in the state in which you are applying for work to be sure that you are aware of all licensing requirements.

Always be sure that all of the information you list is completely accurate. Locate copies of your licenses and certificates and check the exact date and name of the accrediting agency. Use the following worksheet to list your licenses and certificates.

CERTIFICATES AND LICENSES

Name of License _____

Licensing Agency _____

Date Issued _____

Name of License _____

Licensing Agency _____

Date Issued _____

Name of License _____

Licensing Agency _____

Date Issued _____

Professional Memberships and Affiliations

Another potential element in your resume is a section listing professional memberships. Use this section to list involvement in professional associations, unions, and similar organizations. It is to your advantage to list any professional memberships that pertain to the job you are seeking. Be sure to include the dates of your involvement and whether you took part in any special activities or held any offices within the organization. Use the following worksheet to gather your information.

PROFESSIONAL MEMBERSHIPS

Name of Organization _____

Offices Held _____

Activities _____

Date(s) _____

Name of Organization _____

Offices Held _____

Activities _____

Date(s) _____

Name of Organization _____

Offices Held _____

Activities _____

Date(s) _____

Name of Organization _____

Offices Held _____

Activities _____

Date(s) _____

Special Skills

This section of your resume is set aside for mentioning any special abilities you have that could relate to the job you are seeking. This is the part of your resume where you have the opportunity to demonstrate certain talents and experiences that are not central to your educational or work experience. Common examples include fluency in a foreign language, knowledge of a particular style of dance, or proficiency at an additional instrument.

Special skills can encompass a wide range of your talents—remember to be sure that whatever skills you list relate to the type of work you are looking for.

References

References are not usually listed on the resume, but a prospective employer needs to know that you have references who may be contacted if necessary. All that is necessary to include in your resume regarding references is a sentence at the bottom stating, "References are available upon request." If a prospective employer requests a list of references, be sure to have one ready. Also, check with whomever you list to see if it is all right for you to use them as a reference. Forewarn them that they may receive a call regarding a reference for you. This way they can be prepared to give you the best reference possible.

Chapter Two

WRITING YOUR RESUME

*N*ow that you have gathered together all of the information for each of the sections of your resume, it's time to write out each section in a way that will get the attention of whoever is reviewing it. The type of language you use in your resume will affect its success. You want to take the information you have gathered and translate it into a language that will cause a potential employer to sit up and take notice.

Resume writing is not like expository writing or creative writing. It embodies a functional, direct writing style and focuses on the use of action words. By using action words in your writing, you more effectively stress past accomplishments. Action words help demonstrate your initiative and highlight your talents. Always use verbs that show strength and reflect the qualities of a "doer." By using action words, you characterize yourself as a person who takes action, and this will impress potential employers.

The following is a list of verbs commonly used in resume writing. Use this list to choose the action words that can help your resume become a strong one:

administered	introduced
advised	invented
analyzed	maintained
arranged	managed
assembled	met with
assumed responsibility	motivated
billed	negotiated
built	operated
carried out	orchestrated
channeled	ordered
collected	organized
communicated	oversaw
compiled	performed
completed	planned
conducted	prepared
contacted	presented
contracted	produced
coordinated	programmed
counseled	published
created	purchased
cut	recommended
designed	recorded
determined	reduced
developed	referred
directed	represented
dispatched	researched
distributed	reviewed
documented	saved
edited	screened
established	served as
expanded	served on
functioned as	sold
gathered	suggested
handled	supervised
hired	taught
implemented	tested
improved	trained
inspected	typed
interviewed	wrote

Now take a look at the information you put down on the work experience worksheets. Take that information and rewrite it in paragraph form, using verbs to highlight your actions and accomplishments. Let's look at an example, remembering that what matters here is the writing style, and not the particular job responsibilities given in our sample.

WORK EXPERIENCE
Regional Sales Manager

Manager of sales representatives from seven states. Responsible for twelve food chain accounts in the East. In charge of directing the sales force in planned selling toward specific goals. Supervisor and trainer of new sales representatives. Consulting for customers in the areas of inventory management and quality control.

Special Projects: Coordinator and sponsor of annual food industry sales seminar.

Accomplishments: Monthly regional volume went up 25 percent during my tenure while, at the same time, a proper sales/cost ratio was maintained. Customer/company relations improved significantly.

Below is the rewritten version of this information, using action words. Notice how much stronger it sounds.

WORK EXPERIENCE
Regional Sales Manager

Managed sales representatives from seven states. Handled twelve food chain accounts in the eastern United States. Directed the sales force in planned selling towards specific goals. Supervised and trained new sales representatives. Consulted for customers in the areas of inventory management and quality control. Coordinated and sponsored the annual Food Industry Seminar. Increased monthly regional volume 25 percent and helped to improve customer/company relations during my tenure.

Another way of constructing the work experience section is by using actual job descriptions. Job descriptions are rarely written using the proper resume language, but they do include all the information necessary to create this section of your resume. Take the description of one of the jobs your are including on your resume (if you have access to it), and turn it into an action-oriented paragraph. Below is an example of a job description followed by a version of the same description written using action words. Again, pay attention to the style of writing, as the details of your own work experience will be unique.

PUBLIC ADMINISTRATOR I

Responsibilities: Coordinate and direct public services to meet the needs of the nation, state, or community. Analyze problems; work with special committees and public agencies; recommend solutions to governing bodies.

Aptitudes and Skills: Ability to relate to and communicate with people; solve complex problems through analysis; plan, organize, and implement policies and programs. Knowledge of political systems; financial management; personnel administration; program evaluation; organizational theory.

WORK EXPERIENCE
Public Administrator I

Wrote pamphlets and conducted discussion groups to inform citizens of legislative processes and consumer issues. Organized and supervised 25 interviewers. Trained interviewers in effective communication skills.

Now that you have learned how to word your resume, you are ready for the next step in your quest for a winning resume: assembly and layout.

Chapter Three

ASSEMBLY AND LAYOUT

*A*t this point, you've gathered all the necessary information for your resume, and you've rewritten it using the language necessary to impress potential employers. Your next step is to assemble these elements in a logical order and then to lay them out on the page neatly and attractively in order to achieve the desired effect: getting that interview.

Assembly

The order of the elements in a resume makes a difference in its overall effect. Obviously, you would not want to put your name and address in the middle of the resume or your special skills section at the top. You want to put the elements in an order that stresses your most important achievements, not the less pertinent information. For example, if you recently graduated from school and have no full-time work experience, you will want to list your education before you list any part-time jobs you may have held during school. On the other hand, if you have been gainfully employed for several years and currently hold an important position in your company, you will want to list your work experience ahead of your education, which has become less pertinent with time.

There are some elements that are always included in your resume and some that are optional. Following is a list of essential and optional elements:

Essential	*Optional*
Name	Job Objective
Address	Honors
Phone Number	Special Skills
Work Experience	Professional Memberships
Education	Activities
References Phrase	Certificates and Licenses
	Personal Information

Your choice of optional sections depends on your own background and employment needs. Always use information that will put you and your abilities in a favorable light. If your honors are impressive, then be sure to include them in your resume. If your activities in school demonstrate particular talents necessary for the job you are seeking, then allow space for a section on activities. Each resume is unique, just as each person is unique.

Types of Resumes

So far, our discussion about resumes has involved the most common type—the *reverse chronological* resume, in which your most recent job is listed first and so on. This is the type of resume usually utilized in the early stages of a career, such as when one applies to graduate school. The inclusion of dates is optional—and discouraged—in all sections except for the education section, where it is expected.

For someone with a substantial amount of performance experience or varied skills, or for someone looking to change career fields, the *functional resume* may work best. This type of resume focuses more on achievement and less on the sequence of your work history. In the functional resume, your experience is presented by what you have accomplished and the skills you have developed in your past work.

A functional resume can be assembled from the same information you collected for your chronological resume. The main difference lies in how you organize this information. Essentially, the work experience section becomes two sections, with your job duties and accomplishments comprising one section and your employer's name, city, state, your position, and the dates employed making up another section. The first section is placed near the top of the resume, just below the job objective section, and can be called *Accomplishments* or *Achievements.* The second section, containing the bare essentials of your employment history, should come after the accomplishments section and can be titled *Work Experience* or *Employment History*. The other sections of your resume remain the same.

For someone changing careers, emphasis on skills and achievements is essential. The functional resume accomplishes this task. For someone reentering the work force after many years, a functional resume is the obvious choice. If you lack full-time work experience, you will need to draw attention away from this fact and instead focus on your skills and abilities gained possibly through volunteer activities or part-time work. Education may also play a more important role in this resume.

Many performers have multiple and varied skills that correspond to work experience. It is quite common for such actors, singers, directors, and so on to have more than one version of their resume. The order of elements in a resume plays an important part in distinguishing one version from another. Take time to decide which work experience, skills, and information you would like to emphasize in seeking a particular job, and design your resume to suit your needs. An actor seeking a job in film, for example, would not place stage experience before film and industrial experience—although stage experience would still have relevance within the resume.

Which type of resume is right for you will depend on your own personal circumstances. It may be helpful to create a chronological *and* a functional resume and then compare the two to find out which is more suitable.

Layout

Once you have decided which elements to include in your resume and you have arranged them in an order that makes sense and emphasizes your achievements and abilities, then it is time to work on the physical layout of your resume.

There is no single appropriate layout that applies to every resume, but there are a few basic rules to follow in putting your resume on paper:

1. Leave a comfortable margin on the sides, top, and bottom of the page (usually 1 to 1½ inches).

2. Use appropriate spacing between the sections (usually 2 to 3 line spaces are adequate).

3. Be consistent in the *type* of headings you use for the different sections of your resume. For example, if you capitalize the heading EMPLOYMENT HISTORY, don't use initial capitals and underlining for a heading of equal importance, such as Education.

4. Always try to fit your resume onto one page. If you are having trouble fitting all your information onto one

CHRONOLOGICAL RESUME

Michael Alan Pierce
french horn

Address:
145 Main Street #2
Bangor, ME 04322
(207) 555-3236

Member:
American Musicians Guild
American Brass Union
Phi Beta Kappa

Objective
To continue the pursuit of a performance career in orchestral music by gaining admission to the graduate institution of my choice.

Experience

Orchestral

Peabody Symphony Orchestra-Principal	1993-95
Peabody Symphony Orchestra-Asst. Principal	1991-93
Peabody Mixed Brass Choir-Assistant Principal	1991-94
Peabody Opera Orchestra-Principal	1992-95

Chamber

Peabody Chamber Brass-Principal	1993-95
Peabody Chamber Opera Orchestra	1992-94

Awards

Peabody Achievement Award for Graduate Studies	1995
Peabody Concerto Competition-Second Place	1994
St. Stephen's Episcopal Collegiate Scholarship	1991-92

Teachers

Donna Burke-Principal, Portland Symphony	1995-Present
Kadim Shur-Peabody Conservatory of Music	1991-95
Russell Lenhoff-Principal, Boston Lyric Opera	1988-91

Education

Peabody Conservatory of Music, Baltimore, MD.
Bachelor of Music in French Horn Performance, December 1995

FUNCTIONAL RESUME

Kenneth M. Shannon
flute

School Address:
Marks Hall, Room 224
Boulder, CO 80310
(303) 555-3120

Home Address:
45 Long Avenue
Arlington, VA 22202
(703) 555-3574

ORCHESTRAL EXPERIENCE

Professional:
Boulder Summer Wind Quintet (Boulder, CO)
Arlington Civic Orchestra (Arlington, VA)

University of Colorado
at Boulder:
University Festival Orchestra
University Chamber Orchestra
University Winds

Other:
All-State Orchestra (Richmond, VA)
Brandywine Music Camp (Brandywine, MD)
Taft High School Orchestra

HONORS

Taft High School Concerto Competition, First Place
Lavoir Parent Music Achievement Award (Two-year scholarship)

PRIVATE TEACHERS

Dana Goldberg, University of Colorado at Boulder (current teacher)
James Banner, Arlington Symphony Orchestra

EDUCATION

University of Colorado at Boulder School of Music, B. Mus. Flute Performance
(Degree expected in 1998)
Taft High School of the Arts (Graduated June 1994)

page, perhaps you are trying to say too much. Try to edit out any repetitive or unnecessary information or possibly shorten descriptions of earlier jobs. Be ruthless. Maybe you've included too many optional sections. Don't let the idea of having to tell every detail about your life get in the way of producing a resume that is simple and straightforward. The more compact your resume, the easier it will be to read and the better an impression it will make for you.

In some cases, the resume will not fit on a single page, even after extensive editing. In such cases, the resume should be printed on two pages so as not to compromise clarity or appearance. Each page of a two-page resume should be marked clearly with your name and the page number, e.g., "Judith Ramirez, page 1 of 2." The pages should then be stapled together.

Try experimenting with various layouts until you find one that looks good to you. Always show your final layout to other people and ask them what they like or dislike about it, and what impresses them most about your resume. Make sure that is what you want most to emphasize. If it isn't, you may want to consider making changes in your layout until the necessary information is emphasized. Use the sample resumes in this book to get some ideas for laying out your resume.

Putting Your Resume in Print

Your resume should be typed or printed on good quality 8½" × 11" bond paper. You want to make as good an impression as possible with your resume; therefore, quality paper is a necessity. If you have access to a word processor with a good printer, or know of someone who does, make use of it. Typewritten resumes should only be used when there are no other options available.

After you have produced a clean original, you will want to make duplicate copies of it. Usually a copy shop is your best bet for producing copies without smudges or streaks. Make sure you have the copy shop use quality bond paper for all copies of your resume. Ask for a sample copy before they run your entire order. After copies are made, check each copy for cleanliness and clarity.

Another more costly option is to have your resume typeset and printed by a printer. This will provide the most attractive resume of all. If you anticipate needing a lot of copies of your resume, the cost of having it typeset may be justified.

Proofreading

After you have finished typing the master copy of your resume and before you go to have it copied or printed, you must thoroughly check it for typing and spelling errors. Have several people read it over just in case you may have missed an error. Misspelled words and typing mistakes will not make a good impression on a prospective employer, as they are a bad reflection on your writing ability and your attention to detail. With thorough and conscientious proofreading, these mistakes can be avoided.

The following are some rules of capitalization and punctuation that may come in handy when proofreading your resume:

Rules of Capitalization

- Capitalize proper nouns, such as names of schools, colleges, and universities, names of companies, and brand names of products.
- Capitalize major words in the names and titles of books, tests, and articles that appear in the body of your resume.
- Capitalize words in major section headings of your resume.
- Do not capitalize words just because they seem important.
- When in doubt, consult a manual of style such as *Words Into Type* (Prentice-Hall), or *The Chicago Manual of Style* (The University of Chicago Press). Your local library can help you locate these and other reference books.

Rules of Punctuation

- Use a comma to separate words in a series.
- Use a semicolon to separate series of words that already include commas within the series.
- Use a semicolon to separate independent clauses that are not joined by a conjunction.
- Use a period to end a sentence.
- Use a colon to show that the examples or details that follow expand or amplify the preceding phrase.
- Avoid the use of dashes.
- Avoid the use of brackets.
- If you use any punctuation in an unusual way in your resume, be consistent in its use.
- Whenever you are uncertain, consult a style manual.

Chapter Four

THE COVER LETTER

*O*nce your resume has been assembled, laid out, and printed to your satisfaction, the next and final step before distribution is to write your cover letter. Though there may be instances where you deliver your resume in person, most often you will be sending it through the mail. Resumes sent through the mail always need an accompanying letter that briefly introduces you and your resume. The purpose of the cover letter is to get a potential employer to read your resume, just as the purpose of your resume is to get that same potential employer to call you for an interview.

Like your resume, your cover letter should be clean, neat, and direct. A cover letter usually includes the following information:

1. Your name and address (unless it already appears on your personal letterhead).

2. The date.

3. The name and address of the person and company to whom you are sending your resume.

4. The salutation ("Dear Mr." or "Dear Ms." followed by the person's last name, or "To Whom It May Concern" if you are answering a blind ad).

5. An opening paragraph explaining why you are writing (in response to an ad, the result of a previous meeting, at the suggestion of someone you both know) and indicating that you are interested in whatever job is being offered.

6. One or two more paragraphs that tell why you want to work for the company and what qualifications and experience you can bring to that company.

7. A final paragraph that closes the letter and requests that you be contacted for an interview. You may mention here that your references are available upon request.

8. The closing ("Sincerely," or "Yours Truly," followed by your signature with your name typed under it).

Your cover letter, including all of the information above, should be no more than one page in length. The language used should be polite, businesslike, and to the point. Do not attempt to tell your life story in the cover letter. A long and cluttered letter will only serve to put off the reader. If your cover letter is a success, your resume will be read and all pertinent information reviewed by your prospective employer.

Producing the Cover Letter

Cover letters should usually be typed individually, since they are written to particular individuals and companies. You may have been told never to use a form letter for your cover letter. However, form cover letters are acceptable in special cases. For example, if you are an actor sending out a bulk mailing of your photograph and resume, a short, eye-catching biography can serve as an introduction. Such "bios" need not be personalized, even though they are in letter form and are used in the place of a cover letter. Of course, any cover letters you send should be as personal as possible, but don't start from scratch with each one. Create a polished letter you like, and then customize it for each application you submit.

After you have typed your cover letter on quality bond paper, proofread it as thoroughly as you did your resume. Spelling errors are a sure sign of carelessness, and you don't want that to be a part of your first impression on a prospective employer. Handle the letter and resume carefully to avoid any smudges, and then mail both your cover letter and resume in an appropriate sized envelope. Be sure to keep an accurate record of all the resumes you send out and the results of each mailing.

Numerous sample cover letters appear at the end of the book. Use them as models for your own cover letter or to get an idea of how cover letters are put together. Remember, every one is unique and depends on the particular circumstances of the individual writing it and the job for which he or she is applying.

Now the job of writing your resume and cover letter is complete. About a week after mailing resumes and cover letters to potential employers, you will want to contact them by telephone. Confirm that your resume arrived, and ask whether an audition or interview might be possible. Getting your foot in the door during this call is half the battle of a job search, and a strong resume and cover letter will help you immeasurably.

Chapter Five

SAMPLE RESUMES

This chapter contains dozens of sample resumes for people pursuing a wide variety of jobs and careers.

We have included among our samples a few resumes that present the same information in varied formats. These examples, in particular, illustrate the importance of selecting the best layout and design for your circumstances. These samples also represent people with varying amounts of education and experience. Use these samples to model your own resume after. Choose one resume, or borrow elements from several different resumes to help you construct your own.

Tony Williams

232 Forest Avenue
Miami, Florida 33513
(305) 555-5644

PERFORMANCE EXPERIENCE

Orchestral Experience

Florida State University Orchestra
Florida State Band
American World Orchestra

Chamber Music Experience
FSU Contemporary Players (Bass clarinet)
University Jazz Quartet
Willson Quintet

Recitals

Coral Beach Holiday Inn "Holiday Showcase": Dec. 1993-95
Florida-for-the-Arts Young Artist Series: April 1994

Other Experience

Boardwalk Club Piano Bar: Weekly Gig, 1995-Present
    Featuring the Willson Quintet
Interlochen Arts Academy: Summer 1989

TRAINING

Principal Teachers

Clarinet
(Bb and Bass):

Stephen Canby
Geraldine Hicks

Alto Saxophone: Josh Lindberg

Jazz Theory

Josh Lindberg
Renée Gonzales

Master Classes and Coaches

Howard James
Bennie Girbaud
The Davis T. Henderson Quartet

EDUCATION

Florida State Universtiy at Coral Beach 1995
B.A. Music Theory; Music Performance Minor

James Rayburn
baritone

(212) 555-2465

432 E. 55th Street   6' 2", 220 lbs
New York, NY 10011   Light brown hair, Green eyes

OPERA PERFORMANCE

Schaunard, *La Boheme*	Indiana University Opera
Papageno, *The Magic Flute*	Indiana University Opera
Dancairo, *Carmen*	Hammond Symphony
Riff, *West Side Story*	New Horizons Theater

ROLES PREPARED

Figaro, *Le Nozze di Figaro*
Valentin, *Faust*
Harlekin, *Ariadne Auf Naxos* (German and English)

AWARDS

Bel Canto Foundation Competition	Second Place Winner
Metropolitan Opera Competition	Regional Finalist
NATS Competition	First Place Winner

EDUCATION

Indiana University, Bachelor of Music, 1990
Tanglewood Festival, Fellowship Recipient, 1991

Major Teachers: Franz Heidelbeerg, Mariana Petro, James Morrison Eady
Masterclasses: Thomas Garrett, Robert Marks, Renata Teppo

"Mr. Rayburn...negotiated difficult passages with ease and finesse."

"James Rayburn has an energetic...unique style [that] dazzled the audience!"

Ginny Rae Bell
comedienne

510 • 555 • 7382

STAND-UP

Zanies	**Ariel's Big Comics (ABC)**
House of Comedy	**The Funny Farm**
Bay City Backyard	**Cut-Up Club**

COMMERICAL

Little Romeo's West (Restaurant Hostess)	Prince Productions
California Lotto (Woman with Umbrella)	J.B. Hill Inc.

RADIO/TELEVISION

What's So Funny?
College Radio Show   WUCB-UC Berkeley
> • Classic Comedy Routines
> • Call-Ins

Get a Life!
Local Cable Access Show   San Jose Cable Company
> • Stand-Up
> • Human Disinterest Stories
> • Viewer Mail
> • Joke-of-the-Week

SHOWCASE PRODUCTION

A Laugh Riot   House of Comedy, Berkeley, CA
> • Local and Greater West Coast talent
> • Standing room only

Self-Produced comedy showcase. Two nights of stand-up and musical acts at well known comedy club. Contract optioned for 1997-1998

TRAINING

Elaine Fingerhut School for The Comically Insane (Founding member)
Rob Morton Comedy Workshop

University of California at Berkeley
B.A. Political Science. Television and Radio minor

Jennifer T. Modigliano
6342 Rock Creek Road
Stillwater, OK 74800
(405) 555-4323

Objective

To obtain a stage management position in a small theatre company with possible performance opportunities.

Acting Experience

FELICITY/City of Angels / University Theater (University of Oklahoma)
HELENA / All's Well That Ends Well/ University Theater
GINA / The Wild Duck / University Student Theater

Stage Manager Experience

Stage
As You Like It
Spell #7
Three Sisters

Musical
Sweeny Todd / University Theater
Company / University Student Theater
You're a Good Man Charlie Brown / University Student Theater
The Mikado / University Student Theater

Additional Experience

Assistant Stage Manager / University Theater / Two years
Set Designer's Workshop / Three years
Costume Shop / Two years

Modern Dance Classes / Five semesters
The Tonsiltones / female a capella group / Three years
The Laugh Machine / Comedy Improvisation / One year

Education

University of Oklahoma at Tulsa / B.A. Degree expected December 1997

CAREN WILSON
VOCALIST

222 CENTRAL AVE. BATON ROUGE, LA 70822 504/555-4788

CLUBS

CAPETOWN MINES
CAJUN CATIES
JAZZ ETCETERA
FORREST HICKS/HOME OF THE BLUES
CASA DE JAZZ
FIGURE EIGHT CLUB
CATFISH CLUB

SHOWCASE

CLEOPATRA'S GIRLS
GET UP AND SING
ONE NIGHT IN TUNISIA

SHOWS

JELLY'S LAST JAM	TEA ROSE THEATRE
AIN'T MISBEHAVIN'	TEA ROSE THEATRE
PO'	CHERIE PLAYHOUSE
FOR YOUR EYES ONLY	TEA ROSE THEATRE
CHURCHMOUSE CHARLIE	CHERIE PLAYHOUSE

CHOIRS

LOUISIANA GOSPEL CHOIR (1995 GRAMMY WINNERS)
WILSON TRIO (FAMILY GOSPEL TRIO)
MT. VERNOR BAPTIST CHURCH CHOIR

LEN MASADA, Guitar

124 W. Burnside
Hazlet, NJ 07730
(908) 555-2454   (908) 555-2455 (Fax)

Performance Experience/Classical

Bella Aura Trio

- Classical Guitar Trio. Founded 1990.
- Trio has performed throughout New York
  Metropolitan Area, Tristate Region and Suburbs.
- Originally conceived as part of University
  Theatre Arts Program, New York University.

Solo Performances

- Recital at Third Presbyterian, Orange, NJ
- Recital for National Renaissance Week, Hoboken, NJ
- *King John's Faire* (Renaissance Fair) Pallisades, NJ

Popular Experience

Mike Mike

- Five Member Funk and Dance Band, electric guitar
- Weekly Gig at "House of Funk"
- Shows throughout New York and New Jersey

Recordings

With *Bella Aura Trio*

- Bella Aura Trio (Debut Album)   Reno Records
- Bella Aura Trio: Sweete Love   EMI Records, Inc.
- Bella Aura: New Beginnings   Sony Classical

With *Mike Mike*

- I'm Not Crazy (Yet)   MCA Records, Inc.

Althea Morris

433 8th Street
Atlanta, GA 30312
(404) 555-4655 (Service)

COMMERCIAL/JINGLE

Atlanta Bell	Fantastic Travel
Atlanta Cable	MATRIX
Century 21	Georgia Peaches
Harlan Ford	Canape Waterbeds
Jewell Foodstores	Tidy Diaper Service
MacGruders Groceries	*Atlanta Gazette*
Matress Etcetera	East Point Cadillac

INDUSTRIAL/VOICE OVER

Popeye's	In-house
Metropollitan Cable Company	In-house
Wilson Pools Ltd.	Cooper-Wells Inc.

MUSICAL THEATRE

Ensemble member of the Southern and Southwestern touring companies of *Showboat*, 1994-1996

EDUCATION/TRAINING

B.A. American and European History - Spelman College

AGENT

Lana Harris Artists Inc.
55 Continental Drive
Atlanta, Georgia 30301
(404) 555-4100

Carol Lee

1816 Birch Street
Chevy Chase, MD 20045
301-555-4688

Objective   A full-time position as a vocal accompanist at a well
respected music conservatory.

Education   B.M. Vocal Accompaniment Program, Peabody
Conservatory of Music, 1990.

Experience

Private studio lessons
Accompanied three vocal studios with a minimum of fifteen
students each at the undergraduate and graduate level.

- Shared responsibilities as accompanist with two fellow
pianists and accompanist majors.

- Accompanied fifteen to twenty half hour lessons per week.

- Held coaching sessions for a total of thirty hours per week.

Recitals

- Played approximately twenty-five recitals per year as part
of the accompanist program (unpaid).

- Offered additional coachings in preparation for recital.

Opera
- Coached ten graduate voice majors as part of the opera
studio program.

- Substituted for faculty accompanist during absence.

- Assisted the director in scene preparation.

David Atkins
Countertenor

122 S. Chaswell
Hoboken, NJ 07030
(201) 555-4595

CONCERT APPEARANCES

MESSIAH	Handel	Marks Hall-NYC
GLORIA	Vivaldi	New Jersey Choral Society
CATATA No. 140	Mozart	Millard College of Music
MESSIAH	Handel	Millard College of Music
ISRAEL IN EGYPT	Handel	Millard College of Music

RECITAL

HERMIT SONGS	Barber	Hoboken Arts League
LET US GARLANDS BRING	Finzi	Millard College of Music
EXULTATE, JUBILATE	Mozart	Hoboken Arts League
AH, LO PREVIDI! K.272	Mozart	Millard College of Music

OPERATIC ROLES

ACIS	*Acis and Galatea*	Trenton Lyric Opera
AENEAS	*Dido and Aeneas*	New Jersey Opera
FLORIO	*Ascanio in Alba*	Millard College of Music

AWARDS

The Frederick E. Stern Award for Historical Performance Studies
Millard Performance Scholarship

FUTURE ENGAGEMENTS

ACHSAS	*Joshua*	New Jersey Opera
Requiem	Mozart	New Jersey Choral Society

TRAINING

Voice:	Jonathan Rudman, Carol Jonas
Historical Performance:	Eileen Hillman, Thomas McCall, Alan Meeks

Master of Music In Voice Performance, Millard College of Music, NJ
Bachelor of Music in General Music, Piano Concentration, Millard College

DANICA HARRIS
COLORATURA SOPRANO

508 9TH STREET • BROOKLYN, NY 11215 • (718) 555-3735

HEIGHT: 5'2"   HAIR/EYES: BROWN
WEIGHT: 120   BIRTHDATE: 6/1/70

ROLES PERFORMED

THE MAGIC FLUTE	QUEEN OF THE NIGHT	BROOKLYN OPERA	1994
THE ITALIAN GIRL IN ALGIERS	ELVIRA	BROOKLYN OPERA	1993
TALES OF HOFFMAN	OLYMPIA	MADISON OPERA	1992
STREET SCENE	MRS. FIORENTINO	MADISON OPERA	1992
SISTER ANGELICA	FIRST NOVICE	MADISON OPERA	1991
THE PIRATES OF PENZANCE	MABEL	MADISON THEATER	1990
WEST SIDE STORY	MARIA	BLUE LAKE (WI)	1988
THE APPLE GROVE	GIRL	BLUE LAKE	1988

CONCERT AND ORATORIO

FAURÉ REQUIEM	SOLOIST	TRENTON, NJ	1992
CARMINA BURANA	SOLOIST	MADISON, WI	1992
BACH ST. JOHN PASSION	SOLOIST	MADISON, WI	1991
MESSIAH	SOLOIST	MILWAUKEE, WI	1990

TRAINING

TEACHERS	COACHES	INSTRUMENTS	DANCE
EDWARD ELSTON	JOHN BERGERON	PIANO	BALLET
MARCIA CRAWFORD	ROGER THOMAS	ORGAN	JAZZ
ELSIE PITTS	KELLY O'ROURKE	FLUTE	TAP

EDUCATION

MADISON CONSERVATORY OF MUSIC, MADISON, WI
B. M. VOCAL PERFORMANCE, 1992

Christiana Lorca

609 Kirwan Avenue - Newton, MA - 02125 - (508) 555-4382

EDUCATION
Bachelor of Fine Arts, Dance 1995
University of Vermont, Alpine Ridge, VT

ACADEMIC HONORS
and AWARDS
Academic and Talent Scholarships, University of Vermont, 1991-1995
Alpine National Honor Society, Dean's List, Vt. State Academy Scholar

DANCE EXPERIENCE
- **1995**
Falmouth Festival of Music and Art, Francine Denk
Excerpts form *Barcarole*, Jared Lima
Dances of Pearl, Elizabeth Karrol
Golden Slumbers, Lin Hong, Reconstructed by Tani Arroyo
- **1994**
Suite from *Hallowed Eve*, Jared Lima
Heart of Hearts, Susan Nitz
Dream In Red, Tani Arroyo
- **1993**
Lady Sings the Blues, Rena Hartmann
gyroscope, George Lu
synergetic moments, George Lu
- **1986-1990** Lin-Hong Dance Company, Morrisville, VT - Director, Nana Lin-Hong

TEACHING EXPERIENCE
- **1995 to**
present
New England School of Dance, Brockton, MA - Director, Jane Howard
Ballet, Jazz & Tap for children ages 6 to 14
- **1990-1992** Alpine Ridge Dance Center Alpine Ridge, VT - Director, Kristi Buell
Contemporary, Creative Movement and "Baby Steps" for
toddlers and children ages 3 to 13

CHOREOGRAPHIC EXPERIENCE
- **1995**
a rose touched by the sun
Navajo Windsong, Co-choreographed with Rebecca Sherman
- **1993**
Donovan's Dream

Christiana Lorca
609 Kirwan Avenue - Newton, MA - 02125 - (508) 555-4382

page 2

FORMS STUDIED	Ballet, Pointe, Jazz, Tap, Character, Modern/Contemporary, Improvisation, Pom Pons, Synchronized Swimming
TEACHERS	Jared Lima, Tani Arroyo, George Lu, Rena Hartmann, Cynthia Beckett, Kristi Buell, Allen Bounty, Elizabeth Karrol, Darin Alton, Nana Lin-Hong
OTHER EXPERIENCE	New Hampshire Summer Arts Program, West Newton, NH American Student Dance Conference, Middlebury, CT Alpine Ridge Summer Dance Workshops, Alpine Ridge, VT

REFERENCES

Jared Lima
c/o University of Vermont
Wagner Hall, School of Dance
Alpine Ridge, VT 05708

Rena Hartmann
c/o University of Vermont
Wagner Hall, School of Dance
Alpine Ridge, VT 05708

Nana Lin-Hong
Director, Lin-Hong Dance Co.
11 Thompson Street
Morrisville, VT 05722

STEPHANIE T. CORMAN

Double Bass

<table>
<tr><td>

HOME ADDRESS
2565 Cooper Avenue
San Francisco, CA 93120
613-555-4788
</td><td>

SCHOOL ADDRESS
114 E. 23rd Street #16B
New York, NY 10018
212-555-0213
</td></tr>
</table>

EDUCATION AND TRAINING

Juilliard School of Music
    Bachelor of Music: Double Bass Performance with Vaughan Chambers
    Secondary Cello Studies with Denise Novello
    Date of Graduation: May 1996

Private study with Robert Pytorski: San Francisco, California
    Principal Double Bassist, San Francisco Symphony
    Dates of study: September, 1988 -July, 1992, Summer 1989

PROFESSIONAL ORCHESTRAL EXPERIENCE

Greenwich, NY Symphony Orchestra: principal	1994-present
San Francisco Symphony Orchestra	1995
Mt. Vernon, NY Chamber Players	1992-1994

OTHER ORCHESTRAL EXPERIENCE

Juilliard Chamber Orchestra: principal	1995-present
Juilliard Contemporary Ensemble: assistant principal	1993-present
Juilliard Orchestra: assistant principal	1992-present
San Francisco All-City Orchestra	1991-1992

REFERENCES

References are available upon request.

DONNY BEALE
ACTOR
SAG/AFTRA

20 W. Adams Avenue
Hoboken, NJ 07021

Ht: 5'7"   Wt: 135
Hair: Dark Brown   Eyes: Blue

THEATRE

CARRIE'S NIGHTMARE	Jon	Grove Theatre
TRAVESTIES	Ernest	New English Theatre
WISHFUL THINKING	Sam/Host	Grove Theatre
WALTER'S SECRET LIFE	Walter Mitty	Theatre on Hudson
THE ANN DAVIS STORY	Hotel Patron	Spin City Playhose

FILM

DIXIE LILY	Bartender	Fox Entertainment
W.C. FIELDS LIVES	Concierge	Turner Television
JEWEL OF THE NILE	Cab Driver	Paramount Studios

COMMERCIALS

NEW YORK STATE LOTTO	Don Harper Productions
VIDEO KING	Colgate, Inc.
MATRIX PAPER CO.	In-House
HIGGINS CHEVROLET	Family Productions Co.

MUSICALS

THE KING AND I	King of Siam	Tawny Lane Theatre
LES MISERABLES	Marius	Tawny Lane Theatre
THE SOUND OF MUSIC	Rolf	Sloane Playhouse

TRAINING

ACTING: Jonathan Stull, Fred Zimmer; MOVEMENT: Elaine Iwa

SPECIAL SKILLS

Various dialects/accents, lighting and tech, gymnastics, juggling, softball

Thomas Faye

43 Sanger Ave.
Boulder, CO 39828
(303) 555-0829

Objective: To obtain a summer position as a drama counselor
                      at a performing arts camp.

Experience: Assistant Director
                      Rockwell High School. Boulder, CO.

                      Assisted the director of an award-winning high school
                      theater program. Duties included attendance, rehearsal
                      schedules, props management. Supervised lighting and
                      stage crew.

                      Directed students in individual scenes as a part of
                      advanced acting class curriculum.

                      Counselor/Dramatics specialist
                      Jewish Community Center Day Camps.
                      Rock Creek, CO.

                      Organized theater games and weekly talent shows for kids
                      age 6 to13, in addition to daily counselor duties.

Education: Rockwell High School. Boulder, CO.
                      GPA: 3.6
                      Expected graduation date, June 1999.

Special Skills: Acrobatics, ice skating, skiing, hockey, comedy
                      improvisation, photography, sculpture

References: Manny Zitnik, Director of Theater Arts,
                      Rockwell High School. (303) 555-6674.

                      More available upon request.

DIANNA KURAKO

CONDUCTOR

533 SHARON AVE. #3
MEMPHIS, TN 37402
(615) 555-7441

OPERETTA/MUSICAL THEATER

MOST HAPPY FELLA	MEMPHIS CROWN THEATER
THE STUDENT PRINCE	MEMPHIS CROWN THEATER
DIE FLEDERMAUS (THE BAT)	MEMPHIS CROWN THEATER
THE MIKADO	MEMPHIS SAVOYARDS
THE PIRATES OF PENZANCE	MEMPHIS SAVOYARDS
PATIENCE	MEMPHIS SAVOYARDS
THE YEOMEN OF THE GUARD	MEMPHIS SAVOYARDS
TRIAL BY JURY	MEMPHIS SAVOYARDS
THE GONDOLIERS	UNIVERSITY OF TENNESEE
RUDDIGORE	UNIVERSITY OF TENNESEE

ORCHESTRAL

ADAGIO/BARBER	ORCHESTRA MEMPHIS
RODEO/COPELAND	ORCHESTRA MEMPHIS
MASS/BERNSTEIN (EXCERPTS)	BERNSTEIN FEST/Nashville
L'HISTOIRE DU SOLDAT/STRAVINSKY	UNIVERSITY OF TENNESSE

EDUCATION

CONDUCTING TEACHERS AND COACHES: LARRY BECK, JANICE
HOWE, FRANCO BERETTA, LISLE CARTER

UNIVERSITY OF TENNESSEE CHATTANOOGA, TN
B.A. SOCIOLOGY MAJOR MUSIC MINOR

Carter Henderson
Trombone

5767 Edgemoor Drive
1st Floor
St. Louis, MO   63115
(314) 555-2230

Professional Experience

St. Louis Symphony Orchestra	1993 - present
Brass St. Louis (Founder)	1991 - present
Opera Theatre of St. Louis	1990 - 1994
Missouri Civic Symphony	1988 - 1990

Other Experience

St. Louis Conservatory Opera Orchestra
St. Louis Conservatory Orchestra
St. Louis Conservatory Baroque Ensemble
St. Louis Conservatory Trombone Choir
Aspen Festival Orchestra

Festivals

Ravinia Festival/Stern Institute for Brass and Winds	Highland Park, IL
Aspen Music Festival	Aspen, CO

Education

Bachelor of Music: Trombone Performance
   St. Louis Conservatory, 1988
   Principal Teacher: Partrick Hand

Major Conductors: Sir Alan Weelkes, Samuel Cohn, Desie Hillis-Patel,
   Colin MacKinney, Donald Kimbrough, Majorie Lewin

TRINA WEISSMAN

4918 S. Millard
Lake Persephone, NY 10137
(212) 555-0270

Agent: Don Weissman
(212) 555-0200

Hair: Auburn
Eyes: Brown

Height: 4'10"
Age: 14

STAGE AND MUSICAL THEATER

Joseph and the Amazing...Dreamcoat	Chorus	Shubert Theatre
Annie	Annie	Theatre On the Lake
You're a Good Man Charlie Brown	Lucy	Theatre On the Lake
The Sound of Music	Gretl	Theatre On the Lake
Snow White in the Black Forest	Primrose	Starr Children's Theatre
Alice in Wonderland	Mad Hatter	Starr Children's Theatre
Give My Regards to Broadway	Ms. Hollywood	Starr Children's
TheatreThe King and I	Ensemble	Starr Children's Theatre

COMMERCIAL

Pampers	Searle/Ralston
McDonalds	Ryan McCall Inc.
Barbie Playhouse (3 spots)	Mattell In-house
Captain Crunch (Voiceover)	Frasier Productions Ltd.

TRAINING

Acting: Lana Wood, Danny Zucker - Starr Children's Theatre
Singing: Leslie Goodwin (private), Joyful Noise Children's Chorus (7 years)
Dance: Ballet ,Tap (4 years), Modern (2 years) - Metropolitan School of Dance

SPECIAL SKILLS AND INTERESTS

Songwriting, Creative Writing, Swimming, Diving, Gymnastics, Ice Skating, Drawing

Sarah J. Lindenbaum

Home Address:
152 North Avenue
Wilmette, IL 60122
(847) 555-3388

School Address:
33 Maple Ave.
Ann Arbor, MI 49023
(413) 555-6672

VOCATIONAL
OBJECTIVE:
Cello teaching and performing.

EDUCATION:
University of Michigan School of Music.
Ann Arbor, Michigan. 1989.
Music Education major, Cello Performance minor
Cumulative GPA 3.53. Cello studies with Lottie
Liebman and Jonathan Carter.

LARGE
ENSEMBLES:

University of Michigan Orchestra.
Section principal for guest conductors Jeremy Dial
and Sir George Bishop. 1984-1989.

University Cello Octet. 1986-88.

East Lansing Civic Orchestra. Assistant principal. 1988.

Wilmette Chamber Orchestra. Section principal.
Summers, 1982 - present.

SMALL
ENSEMBLES:

Extensive experience in romantic, modern and contemporary periods as
well as baroque Historical Performance. Coaches include members of the
Nouveau String Quartet and distinguished faculty of the Central Midwest
Music Camp and Lake Forest College in addition to University training.
Co-principal University Chamber Ensemble, 1987-1989.

Beverly Whitfield

61 Sanders Ave. #302
New Haven, CT 07450
(203) 555-1644

Height: 5'3"
Weight: 120
Hair: Dark Brown
Eyes: Hazel
D.O.B. 5/4/76

Stage Experience

Hamlet	Ophelia	Yale University Theater
Wine in the Wilderness	Tommy	Yale Little Theater
Joe Turner's Come and Gone	Molly	Yale University Theater
The Caucasian Chalk Circle	Peasant	Yale University Theater
Love's Labor's Lost	Princess	Yale University Theater
The Children's Hour	Mary	Yale Little Theater

Scenework

The Women	Mary	Yale University Drama
The Taming of the Shrew	Kate	Yale University Drama
A Midsummer Night's Dream	Hermia	Yale University Drama
The Importance of Being Earnest	Cecily	Yale University Drama

Related Experience

Assistant Stage Manager , Yale University Drama (2 years)
Set Designer/Coordinator, Yale University Drama (1 semester)
Costume/Makeup Assistant, Yale Little Theater (3 years)

Education

Yale University:	B.A. in English/Theater emphasis (Degree expected, 1997)
Acting:	Connie Jenkins, Lana Haggen, Jim Beale, Gerald Fuller
Dance:	Ballet, Jazz (2 years each), Folkdance (8 years)

Elia M. Gray
AFTRA

Hair:	Black	**Capri Artists Ltd.**	
Eyes:	Brown	**130 W. 10th Street**	
Height	5'4"	**Suite 302**	
Weight:	120	**New York, NY 10012**	
Vocal:	Mezzo/Alto	**(212) 555-5434**	

FILM

THE JURY	Club Dancer	Universal
BUSINESS AS USUAL	Club Patron	Touchstone
BABY TALK 2	Woman in Park	Warner Brothers

TELEVISION

ONE LIFE TO LIVE	Student	ABC
THE CITY	Bar Patron	ABC
THE MINISTER'S WIFE	Mourner	WNET-Great Performances

THEATRE

LONG AGO AND FAR AWAY	Jantzi	Langston Hughes Theatre
PASSAGE OF TIME	Helen	Pinter Play Theatre
SOLOMON'S SONG	Sheba	National Black Theatre
A MIDSUMMER NIGHT'S DREAM	Puck	Steamboat Summer Stock
CARNIVAL	Ensemble	Steamboat Summer Stock
for colored girls...	Lady in Blue	Columbia University
TWELFTH NIGHT	Viola	Columbia University
SOUTH PACIFIC	Bloody Mary	Aspen Theatre

TELEVISION / RADIO

ARTS WATCH	Host, Writer, Prod.	KSNO-Radio-Aspen
HUMAN INTEREST WEEKLY	Reporter	KSKI-TV-Aspen, CO

STAND-UP COMEDY
The Improv Late Nite, Joujou, The Duplex, Rose's Place, Don't Tell Mama, Waki's,
First Up Comedy Club, The Cellar, Harpo's, The Comedy Room

TRAINING

ACTING:	Joel Cohen Theatre Workshop, NY
	National Black Theatre Institute, NY
	New Artist's Workshop, NY
VOICE/MUSIC:	Aspen Music Festival: Janet Winters, Lyn Troy
B.A. Columbia University	Sociology/Romance Languages

SKILLS
Fluent Spanish, French
Dialects: English, Cockney, French, Italian, Australian, Russian, New York, New
York Jewish, Cartoon/Kids voices

Elia M. Gray
Comedian / Actor
AFTRA

Capri Artists Ltd.
130 W. 10th Street
Suite 302
New York, NY 10012
(212) 555-5434

CLUBS
DON'T TELL MAMA	THE CELLAR
HARPO'S	FIRST UP COMEDY CLUB
THE DUPLEX	JOUJOU
ROSE'S PLACE	THE IMPROV LATE NITE
WAKI'S	EMCEE/METRO CRUISES

FILM
THE JURY	Club Dancer	Universal
BUSINESS AS USUAL	Club Patron	Touchstone
BABY TALK 2	Woman in Park	Warner Brothers

TELEVISION
ONE LIFE TO LIVE	Student	ABC
THE CITY	Bar Patron	ABC
THE MINISTER'S WIFE	Mourner	WNET-Great Performances

TELEVISION / RADIO
ARTS WATCH	Host/Writer/Prod.	KSNO-Radio-Aspen
HUMAN INTEREST WEEKLY	Reporter	KSKI-TV-Aspen, CO

THEATRE
LONG AGO AND FAR AWAY	Jantzi	Langston Hughes Theatre
PASSAGE OF TIME	Helen	Pinter Play Theatre
SOLOMON'S SONG	Sheba	National Black Theatre
SOUTH PACIFIC	Bloody Mary	Aspen Theatre

TRAINING
COMEDY:	Dan Stein Comedy Workshop
	Ellen Goodwin Comedy Binge Workshop
ACTING:	Joel Cohen Theatre Workshop, NY
	National Black Theatre Institute, NY
VOICE/MUSIC:	Aspen Music Festival: Janet Winters, Lyn Troy
B.A. Columbia University	Sociology/Romance Languages

SKILLS
Fluent Spanish, French
Dialects: English, Cockney, French, Italian, Australian, Russian, New York, New York Jewish, Cartoon/Kids voices

MARCUS ANTHONY ALTMONT
MODEL

152 Alannis Road • Minton, Connecticut 06457 • 830/555-2587

Height: 6' 2"
Weight: 190
Hair: Black
Eyes: Brown

Professional Experience

Print
J. Crew
Land's End
Tommy Hilfiger
Abercrombie & Fitch
Saks Fifth Avenue
Clinique for Men
Ralph Lauren Home

Television
Calvin Klein Fragrances
Bally's Total Fitness
New York Public Library
Bilford's Bistro and Brewery
Big Brothers (New York)
YMCA (New York)
Audio Consultants

Film
Connecticut Public Television
When Harry Met Sally (extra)

Education and Training

BA, Performing Arts, University of Connecticut (Storrs)
Modeling: TalentExpress

References Available on Request

Michael Dodge

18 Crestwell Lane
Dubuque, IA 52008
312-555-0980

OBJECTIVE

Position in arts management firm, utilizing skills in organization and performance experience in the field of music.

EDUCATION

Grinnell College, Grinnell, Iowa
B.A. Music, Performance Emphasis (Harp)
Graduated May1996
Principal teacher: Elaine DeNoone

EXPERIENCE

Harvey Hall, Grinnell College. **Head Usher** (2 years) Supervised six ushers for campus performances. Prepared ushering schedule. Ushered for performances.

Grinnell Admissions Office. **Assistant** (2 years) Basic receptionst duties: phones, filing, collating, typing. Assisted and fielded calls for admissions director and staff that varied between 7 and 12 people. **Assistant Supervisor**, Campus Tour staff.

Iowa Symphony Orchestra. **Intern-Publicity** Summer intern for mid-sized symphony orchestra. Assembled press scrapbook, assisted with mass mailings in conjunction with ticket office.

MISCELLANEOUS

Performed as solo, chamber and orchestral harpist. **Competed** in regional and scholastic competitions.

America's #1 College Orchestra, Disneyland, CA. Gave 10 to 15 performances weekly. Attended weekly clinics with various managers and artists.

Peer Counselor, Student Support and Placement Services, Grinnell College.

Tutor, Student/Youth Assistance Program, Grinnell, IA.

INTERESTS

Skiing, swimming, biking, working with children, psychology, art history.

Sabrina Mills

508/555-9845

Height: 5' 5"   Voice: Alto/Belt
Weight: 125   Black Hair
Equity Eligible   Green Eyes

Stage Experience

National Tours

Joseph and the Amazing...	Narrator	Winner, 1996 Fox Award
Jesus Christ Superstar	Mary Magdeline	Revival
Fame! The Musical	Doris Canadian/U.S.	

Professional (Local)

The Pirates Of Penzance	Ruth	Auditorium Theatre
A Little Night Music	Petra	Emerson Theatre
The Wiz (Revival)	Miss One	Apollo Theatre

Miscellaneous

Les Miserables	Eponine	Medford Theater Group
Pippin	Fastrada	Boston U. Players
Cats	Rumpleteaser	Boston College Theater
West Side Story	Teresa	Boston College Theater

Training

Voice (Classical):	Mirella Amato
Belt:	Fran Lieber, Jon Errol
Dance:	Liza Jenkins Studio, Boston

Education

B. F. A. Boston College, 1994

85 Walnut Street • Fairhaven, MA • 02744

Aaron Thomas
bass-baritone

27 Spring Street
Yellow Springs, OH 44052
(216) 555-8763

Opera and Musical Theater

Old Maid & the Thief	Bob	Cleveland Music College
La Boheme	Colline	Cleveland Music College
Le Nozze di Figaro	Antonio	Cleveland Music College
	Figaro (cover)	
The Mikado	Mikado	College Savoyards
Pippin	Charlemaigne	Star Dinner Theater
South Pacific	Emile deBecque	Star Dinner Theater
My Fair Lady	Col. Pickering	Star Dinner Theater

Oratorio

Creation	Haydn	Cleveland College Chorus
Messiah	Handel	Cleveland College Chorus
Magnificat	Bach	Cleveland College Chorus
Judas Maccabeus (excerpts)	Handel	Cleveland College Chorus

Education

Cleveland Music College, Bachelor's Degree: Voice, 1994
Summer Abroad Program: Piazza, Italy, 1992
Teachers: Jane Leeds, Karl Henderson, Cynthia Harding
Dance: Tap (2 years), Jazz (3 years), Modern (1 year)

JACOB LANG

BASS

245 N. ABBOTT DRIVE
BLOOMINGTON, IN 46802
812-555-6144

ROLES PERFORMED

NICK SHADOW	*THE RAKE'S PROGRESS*	INDIANA U. OPERA
COMMENDATORE	*DON GIOVANNI*	INDIANA U. OPERA
CRESPEL	*TALES OF HOFFMAN*	INDIANA U. OPERA
DULCAMARA	*THE ELIXER OF LOVE*	INDIANA U. OPERA

ROLES STUDIED

FAUST	*FAUST*	IU OPERA STUDIO
SARASTRO	*THE MAGIC FLUTE*	IU OPERA STUDIO
HORACE TABOR	*THE BALLAD OF BABY DOE*	IU OPERA STUDIO

THEATER

JIM	*THE GLASS MENAGERIE*	FAIR LAKE ACADEMY
ZACH	*UNTAMED HEART*	FAIR LAKE ACADEMY
CROW	*MR. MONDAY*	FAIR LAKE ACADEMY

EDUCATION

B.M. VOCAL PERFORMANCE - INDIANA UNIVERSITY - DEGREE EXPECTED 1997
HONORS STUDENT - FAIR LAKE ACADEMY - FAIR LAKE, INDIANA
    AREAS OF CONCENTRATION: THEATER & MUSIC
SKILLS: ACTING, DANCE, JUGGLING, STAGE COMBAT
INSTRUMENTS: PIANO, ACOUSTIC GUITAR, SAXOPHONE
OTHER INTERESTS: FOOTBALL, BASEBALL, FILM, RELIGIOUS STUDIES

RENÉE T. GIBSON
BASSOON

Present Address:
145 Main Street #2
Evanston, IL 60602
(847) 555-8103

Home Address:
25 Seponsette Road
Pleasant, NJ 10540
(201) 555-4282

ORCHESTRAL EXPERIENCE:

    Northwestern University Chamber Players - two years
    Northwestern University Orchestra- three years
    Chicago Civic Orchestra - principal two years
    All-State Orchestra - principal four years
    Juilliard Pre-College Orchestra - principal two years
    Tri-State Youth Orchestra - three years

ENSEMBLE EXPERIENCE:

    Northwestern University Wind Ensemble - principal one year
    University Chamber Winds - three years

SPECIAL HONORS:

    Northwestern Concerto Competition, Third Place, 1994
    New York Tri-State Wind Ensemble, principal, 1992
    Leonard Bernstein Festival New England, participant, 1990

PRIVATE TEACHERS:

    Kevin Sheehan, current teacher
    Manfred Geller, principal, Chicago Symphony
    Jonathan Woods, ret. principal, New York Philharmonic

EDUCATION:

    Northwestern University, B. Mus. Bassoon Performance
       (Degree expected in 1995)
    Juilliard Pre-College division, 1986-1990

Martha Garrett, Oboe
68447 Owahu Drive
Honolulu, Hawaii 96732
808-555-4700

Education

B. Mus. (Performance) Cincinatti Institute of Music, 1985

Performing Experience

Associate Principal Oboe, Honolulu Symphony
Principal Oboe, Dayton Philharmonic
Principal Oboe, Ohio Civic Orchestra
Assistant Principal Oboe, Scranton Symphony

Teaching Experience

Associate Professor, Dayton University
Guest Lecturer-College of Wooster; University of Honolulu

Honors

Runner-up Principal Oboe, Cincinatti Orchestra
Finalist Principal Oboe, Philadelphia Symphony

Summer Festivals

Principal Oboe, Spoleto Festival
Fellow, Aspen Music Festival
Fellow, Wildwood Music Festival

Teachers and Conductors

Robert Klein, Principal Oboe, Cincinatti Orchestra
Joseph Cade, Professor of Oboe, Cincinatti Institute of Music
Sarah Bedell, Conductor, Ohio Civic Orchestra
Jachim Andres, Director, Honolulu Youth Symphony

Linda Whitman
Violin

Present Address:
250 Massachusettes Ave. #2
Boston. MA 02115
(617) 555-2204

Home Address:
16 Timber Lane
North Ridge, RI 02904
(303) 555-8785

EDUCATION

New England Conservatory (B.M. to be awarded 1996)
Joachim Meyer, Principal Teacher

ORCHESTRAL ENGAGEMENTS

New England Conservatory Orchestra (co-principal 2nd violin)
Providence Youth Orchestra
Rhode Island All-State Orchestra (concertmaster)
North Ridge High School Orchestra (concertmaster)

CHAMBER MUSIC ENSEMBLES/FESTIVALS

"Sommerville" String Quartet
Tanglewood Music Festival
New England Youth Chamber Arts Program

AWARDS

Lisbon Young Artist Competition, New England Region, Finalist
Concerto Winner, North Ridge High School
North Ridge Scholarship for Arts and Music, Winner

SANDRA MURDOCH, *violinist*

3807 N. California • Chicago, IL 60618 • (312) 555-3837

EDUCATION

New England Conservatory of Music (Boston, MA)
>   Master's degree in Violin Performance (1990)
>   Bachelor's degree in Violin Performance (1987)

St. Louis Conservatory of Music (St. Louis, MO)
>   1985-1987

TRAINING

Principal Teachers: Jonathan Baehr, Gabriel Talon, Jorge Ribas
Coaches: David Lerner, Parnell Gibson, Lottie Spelling, Colin Furth

PERFORMANCE EXPERIENCE

Civic Orchestra of Chicago
Illinois Symphony
New England Conservatory Orchestra
Sarasota Music Festival
Hansen International Festival

TEACHING EXPERIENCE

Merit Music Program (Chicago, IL)
American Conservatory of Music (Chicago, IL)
Sherwood Conservatory (Chicago, IL)
New England Conservatory (Boston, MA)

STUART JAMES
Tuba

134 N. College Park
Rochester, NY 11966
(212) 555-6025

EDUCATION

Bachelor of Music (Tuba Performance)
   Eastman School of Music, 1996
Aspen Festival School, Aspen, Colorado, summer, 1993
Mills High School, Takoma Springs, Washington, 1991

PROFESSIONAL EXPERIENCE

Tubist, The American Wind Ensemble, Rochester, NY,
   presently
Tubist, The New Jersey Chamber Orchestra
Tubist, The Lincoln Brass Quintet, Rochester, NY
   northeast summer tour

OTHER ORCHESTRAL EXPERIENCE

Tubist, The Eastman Orchestra, 1992-1996
Tubist, The Eastman Mixed Choir Orchestra
   West Coast Tour, spring, 1995
Tubist, The Aspen Festival Orchestra, summer, 1993
Tubist, Seattle Youth Symphony, 1988-1991

TEACHERS AND OTHER REFERENCES

Daniel Bowdoin, Principal Tubist, New York State Orchestra
Linwood Miller, Professor of Tuba, Eastman School of Music
Johann Behr, Conductor, Seattle Youth Symphony

Barry Kim
actor/singer
16 Brookfield Road • Hartford, CT 07450 • 203/555-7879

height: 5'7" weight: 135
hair and eyes: black

theater

Much Ado About Nothing	*Claudio*
Our Town	*Tom*
Tom Jones	*Highwayman*

musical theater

The King and I	*The King*
Amahl and the Night Visitors	*Amahl*
The Secret Garden	*Colin*
Pippin	*Charlemaigne*

choral

muscial excerpts:

*Carousel**	*Little Shop of Horrors**
*The Fantasticks**	*South Pacific*
*A Little Night Music**	*The Wiz*

*as soloist

solo classical: *Chichester Psalms (Bernstein)*
Requiem (Fauré)
Requiem (Lloyd Webber)

B. Kim • page 2

education

Ethel Barrymore High School for the Performing Arts
LaFayette, NY
Graduation Date: June 2, 1997

curriculum includes:

Acting	Dance (Ballet, Tap)
Singing	Improvisation
Fencing/Stage Combat	Mime/Character

Hartt Performance Center for Young Artists
Hartford, CT
Summers, 1991 to present

additional training

Private Voice Lessons	2 years	Phillip Theopholis
Private Piano Lessons	5 years	Deanna Harris

related skills/hobbies

Debate and Forensics, Playwriting, Baseball, Hiking, Fishing

references

available upon request

BERNARDO ALTI, COMPOSER

333 Central Park West Apt. 5b   New York, NY 10023   212/555-5876

EDUCATION	**Mannes College of Music**	**Doctor of Musical Arts,** 1995
	The Juilliard School	**Master of Music,** 1992 **Bachelor of Music,** 1991
	The Juilliard School Pre-College Division	Piano Studies 1985-1987
	Marcia Umberto Musical Academy	Piano and Clarinet Studies, 1977-1985

PRINCIPAL TEACHERS	Composition	Master Classes
	Walter Stanley Veronique Pujo Hugh Waldman	Marcia Umberto Jean-Luc Mouton

TEACHING	The Juilliard School	Teaching Assistant in Music Theory, 1990-1992

AWARDS   Merit Scholarship, Mannes College of Music, 1988

Recipient, Leonard Berstein Composition Award, 1991

SKILLS & INTERESTS   Fluent in Spanish and French

Piano, Oboe, Photography, Modern Dance

BERNARDO ALTI, COMPOSER

Page 2

PARTIAL LIST OF COMPOSITIONS

"Divertimento" for Winds and Percussion

"Elias" - Quartet for Woodwinds and Timpani

"Fanfare" for Brass, Timpani and Piano

"Fantasie" for Bb Clarinet, Bass Clarinet and Orchestra

"Lawrence" - Clarinet Concerto

"Magnificat" for Strings, Piano and Women's Chorus

"Our Town" - Overture for Orchestra

Piano Concerto Nos. 1 to 4

Piano Toccata

String Quartet Nos. 1 and 2

"The Troubadour" for Woodwind Quintet and Piano

REFERENCES   Credential File Available:

Placement Office
Mannes College of Music
140 Riverside Drive
New York, NY 10025

Ronald A. Sandler
Trumpet

22 Ridge Avenue
Lexington, MA 02113
(617) 555-3212

Orchestral Engagements

New England Conservatory Orchestra - principal
NEC Opera Orchestra - principal
Hartt Symphony and Opera Orchestras - principal
Tanglewood Festival Orchestra and Chamber Orchestra

Other Ensembles

NEC Honors Brass Quintet
NEC Wind Ensemble
Hartt Jazz Ensemble
Hartt Contemporary Players

Recital

Jordan Hall First Night, Boston, MA (NEC) - benefit for renovation
Second Presbyterian Church, Lexington, MA
St. Augusta Church, Hartford, CT

Awards

New England Conservatory Graduate Award
Hartt School of Music Performance Scholarship
Tanglewood Festival Performance Scholarship

Education

New England Conservatory of Music - M.M. 1992
Hartt School of Music - B.M. 1990
Teachers: Rudolph Blintz, Boston Symphony Orchestra
           Mason Friml - Amercian Symphony
           Garbriel Thompson - Canadian Brass Quintet

Sandy Miles
musician

823 Lima Drive • Rio Valley, CA 94663 • 415/555-4877

Performance experience

Choral
- **Rio Valley High School Mixed Choir (4 years)**
- **Rio Valley High School Girls Choir (2 years)**
- **Rio Valley High School Show Choir (3 years)**
- **Rio Valley High School Madrigal Chorus (2 years)**

Band
- **Rio Valley High School Orchestra**
- **Rio Valley High School Marching Band**

Teaching experience

- **Echo Park Pro Musica (Redding, CA)**
Counselor, junior league
- **Private studio - vocal coaching**

Teachers

Voice:	**Trudy Berger, James Davidson**
Trumpet:	**John Biggs**
Piano:	**Mary Jane Howe**

Awards

Rio Valley High School Music Achievement Award
Scholarship Receipient - Echo Park Pro Musica

ALANA BERRY - LYRIC COLORATURA

333 E. Stadium Drive • Kalamazoo, MI 49007 • (616) 555-3735

Height: 5'2"

Weight: 130

Hair and Eyes: Brown

Age Range: 12 - 35

OPERA AND OPERETTA

THE ELIXER OF LOVE	ADINA	Western Michigan Univ.
THE MAGIC FLUTE	FIRST LADY (PAMINA cover)	WMU
COSI FAN TUTTE	DESPINA	WMU
THE NIGHT WATCHMAN	LADY CLAIRE	Kalamazoo Carr Theater
THE IMPRESARIO	MME. TRILLO	WMU
VIVA LA MAMMA!	LUIGIA	Kalamazoo College
THE YEOMEN OF THE GUARD	ELSIE	WMU

CONCERT

CARMINA BURANA	SOLOIST	Carr Concert Series
FAURÉ REQUIEM	SOLOIST	WMU Chamber Singers
MESSIAH	SOLOIST	WMU Comm. Chorus

TRAINING

TEACHERS	*COACHES*	*SPECIAL SKILLS*
Rose D'Angelou	Kelly Logan	Piano, Guitar
Thomas Bickel	Libby Jonas	Ballet, Jazz
Nancy Edelman	Don Fried	Acting, Children's Theater

EDUCATION

WESTERN MICHIGAN UNIVERSITY, M.M. (Opera Performance): Expected 1994

WESTERN MICHIGAN UNIVERSITY, B. A. (Music Performance: Voice) 1992

KALAMAZOO COLLEGE Pre-College Music and Arts Program, 1984-1988

REFERENCES Available upon request

ALANA BERRY

333 E. Stadium Drive • Kalamazoo, MI 49007 • (616) 555-3735

Height: 5'2"   **Hair and Eyes:** Brown
Weight: 130   **Age Range:** 12 - 35

MUSICAL THEATER

THE SOUND OF MUSIC	MARIA	Kalamazoo Carr Theater
A LITTLE NIGHT MUSIC	ANNE	WMU
LITTLE SHOP OF HORRORS	RONNETTE	WMU
SWEENY TODD	JOANNA	WMU
PIPPIN	CATHERINE	Kalamazoo College

OPERA

THE ELIXER OF LOVE	ADINA	Western Michigan Univ.
THE MAGIC FLUTE	FIRST LADY (PAMINA cover)	WMU
COSI FAN TUTTE	DESPINA	WMU
THE IMPRESARIO	MME. TRILLO	WMU

ROLES PREPARED

THE BALLAD OF BABY DOE	BABY DOE	WMU
MANON	MANON	WMU
DER ROSENKAVELIER	SOPHIE	WMU
DON GIOVANNI	ZERLINA	WMU

TRAINING

TEACHERS AND COACHES:	Rose D'Angelou, Thomas Bickel, Libby Jonas
ACTING:	Nancy Edelman, Paul Frisch
DANCE:	Ballet, Jazz, Ballroom
DIRECTOR:	Children's Theater, Kalamazoo Carr Theater
INSTRUMENTS:	Piano, Guitar

EDUCATION

WESTERN MICHIGAN UNIVERSITY, M.M. (Opera Performance): Expected 1994
WESTERN MICHIGAN UNIVERSITY, B. A. (Music Performance: Voice) 1992
KALAMAZOO COLLEGE Pre-College Music and Arts Program, 1984-1988

REFERENCES Available upon request

Jerome Anthony Smith

Hair: Brown   Eyes: Brown   Height: 6 ft. 2 in.   Weight: 180 lbs.

TEACHERS

Sergei Borga	Tucson, Arizona
Joi Noble, Ty Hind	Pittsburgh, Pennsylvania
Esther Jing-Carr	Toledo, Ohio

PROFESSIONAL EXPERIENCE

1984-87	Toledo Dance Co. corps de ballet	Director: Joshua Banks
1985-86	Ballet Midwest corps de ballet	Director: Richard Rounder
1986-88	Pennsylvania Ballet corps de ballet	Director: Benjamin George
1988-91	Arizona Ballet soloist	Director: Pasha Ronan
1991-92	National Ballet Theatre soloist	Director: Henry Davison

Since 1992 I have maintained guest artist contracts with the following companies:

Utah Ballet	Director: Margo Vitrella
Portland City Ballet	Director: Marni Beaty
Houston Ballet	Director: Carl Heinreiksen
Pittsburgh Ballet	Director: Shari Tilson-Myer
Lake Erie Ballet	Director: Renee Rosen

SIGNIFICANT ACCOMPLISHMENTS

In 1993 I originated the role of Thomkin in Sergei Borga's ballet *Anatomy of a Nation*. Later that year I appeared in a photographic essay of the production in *Dance Today*. I am featured in the short film *Dancin' Up to Heaven*, and was interviewed for *Dance!America*, a documentary film commemorating the anniversary of the National Ballet Theatre. An original composition, *Life Without Wings*, was also featured in the film. This piece later received the Mark Award for Excellence.

Jerome Anthony Smith
page 2 of 2

REPERTOIRE

American Symphony	Noel
Carmina Burana	Oiseau de l'Orange
Cinderella	Romeo and Juliet
Firebird	Rosa Lee Pas de Deux
Gigi	Serenade
La Jolite	Sleeping Beauty
Life Without Wings	Swan Lake
Merry Widow	Symphony in C
Nutcracker	Western Song

TEACHING ENGAGEMENTS

Portland City Ballet	Portland, OR
Pittsburgh Ballet	Pittsburgh, PA
National Ballet Theatre	Washington, DC
Toledo Dance Company	Toledo, OH
Ballet Midwest	Dayton, OH
Arizona Regional Ballet	Tucson, AZ
Filbert Junior College	Filbert, UT
Austin Concert Ballet	Austin, TX
Arise Dance Theatre	Salt Lake City, UT
Utah Regional Ballet	Provo, UT

CHOREOGRAPHY

Life Without Wings	National Ballet Theatre
Allegro in D	Austin Concert Ballet

Natalie Herrera

3630 N. Greenview

Chicago, IL 60614

(312) 555-2610

Personal Information

Height 5'3", Weight 105 lbs., Hair and Eyes dark brown

Training

Ballet:

Lehmann School of Ballet, Chicago

Ruth Page School of Dance, Chicago

Howard Davis Studio, New York City

Jamie Chung Studio, New York City

Walter Raines, Alvin Ailey School, New York City

Modern:

Penny Paretsky, Ricardo Ribera Dance Etcetera

Denise Jefferson Harper, Alvin Ailey School

Maria Bryant, Hartt Technique, Alvin Ailey School

Jazz:

Joel Hall, Joel Hall Studio, Chicago

Lou Conte, Hubbard Street Dance Chicago

Martin Stone, Ed Sullivan Studios, New York City

Herrera, p.2

Credits

    Soloist, Joel Hall Dancers

    Soloist, Ricardo Ribera Dance Etcetera

    Soloist, Ballet Latina, Christina Fernandez, New York City

    Soloist, Lamplight Dinner Theatre, "That's Dancin'!"

    Soloist, Nutcracker, Danse Arabe, Highland Park Civic

    Soloist, Nutcracker, corps de ballet, Waltz of the Flowers,
        Lehmann School

    Soloist, Cinderella, Lehmann School

Choreography

    La Valse, Maurice Ravel, Joel Hall, reviewed in
        ***Dance Today*, June, 1988**

    Java Jive, Manhattan Transfer, jazz presentation

    Brazilian Nights, jazz solo, Ed Sullivan Studios

    Hot and Now, jazz review, Ricardo Ribera Dance Etcetera

    Bloomfield Ballet, jazz dance workshop, Devin Diamanti,
        Bloomfield, IL

    Westmont Ballet Studio, ballet workshop, Westmont, NJ

Laralynn Jennings
234 Mapletree Avenue
Baltimore, MD 21216
410-555-5478

Date of Birth: 6/3/73
Height: 5'4"
Education: BFA in Dance with honors, University of Maryland, Dec., 1995

Dance Experience:

University of Maryland Dance Company

Don't Just Stand There (Tessa Michel)
Tucan Sam Tango (T. R. Jamison)- duet
Give Me an 'A ' (Alan Bond)
To Misha, With Love (Rubix) - Amor
Young Blood (Chinoo Patel)

American Dance Theatre

Stars and Stripes (Ballanchine)
Gigi (Lunaire) - Gigi
Rodeo (Agnes de Mille)
The Nutcracker (Petipa) - Dance of the Reed Pipes

Ontario Reperetory Ballet
Cinderella (Petipa) - Wicked Stepmother

Training:

University of Maryland (1991-1995)
Ballet: Mira Browning, Giselle Martinique
Modern: Bartholo Jenkins, Adam Coles, Jeannie Jones

Rosario Dance Studio (1984-1991)
Ballet, Jazz, Tap, Modern, Character & Mime

American Academy of Ballet Arts (1980-1984)
Ballet: Alicia Doggett

Laralynn Jennings
page two

Master Classes/Workshops

Ballet	Modern	Jazz
Cathy Burnett	Tory Spencer	Bobby Cort
Liza Greene	Alana Parsons	Tricia Latman
Darius Michaels	Sibarus Dean	
Joseph Pincus		

Teaching Experience: (Beginner to Adult Advanced)

Dance Baltimore (1993-1995): Ballet & Jazz
Roasario Dance Studio (1991-1994): Ballet, Tap, Modern
Private teaching (1992-1995): Ballet, Modern, Tap & Character

Scholarships/Awards:

The Roosevelt Foundation Scholarship
The University of Maryland Foundation Scholarship
The Martina Zotto Scholarship (University of Maryland)
Washingon School of the Arts Summer Program
Silver Spring School of Ballet Summer Program

References:

Mira Browning
The University of Maryland
14 Brown Hall
Baltimore, MD 21208

Tessa Michel
The University of Maryland
14 Brown Hall
Baltimore, MD 21208

More available upon request

Laralynn Jennings
234 Mapletree Avenue
Baltimore, MD 21216
410-555-5478

Date of Birth: 6/3/73
Height: 5'4"
Education: BFA in Dance with honors, University of Maryland, Dec., 1995

Dance Experience:

<u>University of Maryland Dance Company</u>

Don't Just Stand There (Tessa Michel)
Tucan Sam Tango (T. R. Jamison)- duet
Give Me an 'A ' (Alan Bond)
To Misha, With Love (Rubix) - Amor
Young Blood (Chinoo Patel)

<u>American Dance Theatre</u>

Stars and Stripes (Ballanchine)
Gigi (Lunaire) - Gigi
Rodeo (Agnes de Mille)
The Nutcracker (Petipa) - Dance of the Reed Pipes

<u>Ontario Reperetory Ballet</u>
Cinderella (Petipa) - Wicked Stepmother

Training:

<u>University of Maryland</u> (1991-1995)
Ballet: Mira Browning, Giselle Martinique
Modern: Bartholo Jenkins, Adam Coles, Jeannie Jones

<u>Rosario Dance Studio</u> (1984-1991)
Ballet, Jazz, Tap, Modern, Character & Mime

<u>American Academy of Ballet Arts</u> (1980-1984)
Ballet: Alicia Doggett

Laralynn Jennings
page two

Master Classes/Workshops

Ballet	Modern	Jazz
Cathy Burnett	Tory Spencer	Bobby Cort
Liza Greene	Alana Parsons	Tricia Latman
Darius Michaels	Sibarus Dean	
Joseph Pincus		

Teaching Experience: (Beginner to Adult Advanced)

Dance Baltimore (1993-1995): Ballet & Jazz
Roasario Dance Studio (1991-1994): Ballet, Tap, Modern
Private teaching (1992-1995): Ballet, Modern, Tap & Character

Scholarships/Awards:

The Roosevelt Foundation Scholarship
The University of Maryland Foundation Scholarship
The Martina Zotto Scholarship (University of Maryland)
Washingon School of the Arts Summer Program
Silver Spring School of Ballet Summer Program

References:

Mira Browning
The University of Maryland
14 Brown Hall
Baltimore, MD 21208

Tessa Michel
The University of Maryland
14 Brown Hall
Baltimore, MD 21208

More available upon request

Michael Alan Pierce
french horn

Address:
145 Main Street #2
Bangor, ME 04322
(207) 555-3236

Member:
American Musicians Guild
American Brass Union
Phi Beta Kappa

Objective   To continue the pursuit of a performance career in orchestral music by gaining admission to the graduate institution of my choice.

Experience

Orchestral

Peabody Symphony Orchestra-Principal	1993-95
Peabody Symphony Orchestra-Asst. Principal	1991-93
Peabody Mixed Brass Choir-Assistant Principal	1991-94
Peabody Opera Orchestra-Principal	1992-95

Chamber

Peabody Chamber Brass-Principal	1993-95
Peabody Chamber Opera Orchestra	1992-94

Awards

Peabody Achievement Award for Graduate Studies	1995
Peabody Concerto Competition-Second Place	1994
St. Stephen's Episcopal Collegiate Scholarship	1991-92

Teachers

Donna Burke-Principal, Portland Symphony	1995-Present
Kadim Shur-Peabody Conservatory of Music	1991-95
Russell Lenhoff-Principal, Boston Lyric Opera	1988-91

Education

Peabody Conservatory of Music, Baltimore, MD.
Bachelor of Music in French Horn Performance, December 1995

Kenneth M. Shannon
flute

School Address:
Marks Hall, Room 224
Boulder, CO 80310
(303) 555-3120

Home Address:
45 Long Avenue
Arlington, VA 22202
(703) 555-3574

ORCHESTRAL EXPERIENCE

Professional: Boulder Summer Wind Quintet (Boulder, CO)
                  Arlington Civic Orchestra (Arlington, VA)

University of Colorado
  at Boulder: University Festival Orchestra
                  University Chamber Orchestra
                  University Winds

Other: All-State Orchestra (Richmond, VA)
                  Brandywine Music Camp (Brandywine, MD)
                  Taft High School Orchestra

HONORS

Taft High School Concerto Competition, First Place
Lavoir Parent Music Achievement Award (Two-year scholarship)

PRIVATE TEACHERS

Dana Goldberg, University of Colorado at Boulder (current teacher)
James Banner, Arlington Symphony Orchestra

EDUCATION

University of Colorado at Boulder School of Music, B. Mus. Flute Performance
    (Degree expected in 1998)
Taft High School of the Arts (Graduated June 1994)

CAROL M. LOOMIS

85 Peace Drive
Portland, OR 97219
(503)555-0186

OBJECTIVE: A part-time position as a dance instructor that will enable me to attend classes while working with children.

EDUCATION: June 1994 Graduate of Lakeside High School
Portland, OR
GPA 3.00/4.00

In Fall 1994, I will attend Lewis and Clark College in Portland, OR. I will graduate in 1998 with a Bachelor's degree in Dramatic Arts.

WORK EXPERIENCE: Assistant Dance Instructor
The Dance Studio, Portland, OR

Responsibilities: teaching tap and jazz to school-aged children.
Summers 1992, 1993

SPECIAL SKILLS: Two-year member of 4-H club
Four years jazzercize
Six years tap and ballet lessons
I am a very diligent and friendly dance instructor

REFERENCES: Cathy Delude, dance instructor, The Dance Studio
555-1154
Norman Haney, family friend
555-7600

Joshua K. Peck
301 Coates Drive
International Falls, MN 56649
(218)555-2452

Objective: To become an actor in a community theater.

Acting Experience: Member of the Drama Club for four years.

Acted in "The People vs Maxine Loe," my senior year in High School.

Work Experience:
June 1993
to Present

McDonald's Restaurant
International Falls, MN

Responsibilities: operate cash register, improve and maintain the site and lobby, make fries, cook the food, and close the restaurant at night.

June 1992
to August 1992

Taco Bell Restaurant
International Falls, MN

Responsibilities: operated electronic cash register, prepared and packaged the food, and cleaned and maintained restaurant.

Personal: Competed in track and field for six years. I was a multi-event winner and team captain my senior year.

Member of the football team for two years: 1992, 1993.

Fluent in written and conversational French.

Education: Graduated from International Falls High School in 1993

Social Studies award winner.

Plan to attend St. Cloud State University in St. Cloud, MN in 1994. I will major in Speech/Communication/Theater Education and will graduate in 1998.

References: Available upon request.

Daniel M. Redding

presently at
222 Washington Ave.
Sommerville, MA 02181
617-555-1188

permanently at
400 E. LaSalle Drive
Milwaukee, WI 53211
515-555-0212

Baccalaureate 1994. Boston University, Boston., MA
Matriculated 1990, Harvey Mudd School, Racine, WI
Post-graduate studies, Boston University

• **Assistant Stage Manager:** *Milwaukee Light Opera (1993 season)*; Managed the season run of two Light Opera and Operetta productions. Assisted the stage mananger in preparation for over forty other performances in the full season repertory.

• **Organist and Cantor:** *Grace Lutheran Church, Cedar Bluff, WI* (1989-90); Served as organist for weekly services and major festival and holidays. I organized and participated in special services invloving other professional and volunteer musicians.

• **Tenor Soloist, Substitute Organist and Music Director:** *Canton Presbyterian Church, Canton, MA (1991-1994)*; Assisted in musical selection and preparation of professional (paid) quartet in which I sang tenor. At various times throughout my tenure, I was called upon to substitute for the director both as organist and conducting from the console.

• **Sales Representative:** *Milwukee Symphony Chorus, Milwaukee, WI (Summers 1991, 1992)* Representative in telephone sales and ticket subscription renewal. Served as assistant-coordinator of the phone drive in addition to other duties in 1992.

• **Office Assistant:** *Boston University Admissions Office (Sept. 1991-May 1994)*; General office work included reception, filing, word processing (Microsoft Word) and database programming (FileMaker Pro).

• **Chorister:** *Milwukee Symphony Chorus, Boston University Choir, Boston University Singers, The Longy Chamber Singers, Boston University Opera Chorus, Grace Lutheran Choir, Canton Presbyterian Choir, Wisconson Honors Chorus.*

references furnished upon request

Daniel M. Redding

presently at
222 Washington Ave.
Sommerville, MA 02181
617-555-1188

permanently at
400 E. LaSalle Drive
Milwaukee, WI 53211
515-555-0212

Organ Experience

• **Organist and Cantor:** *Grace Lutheran Church, Cedar Bluff, WI* (1989-90); I served as organist for weekly services and major festival and holidays. I organized and participated in special services invloving other professional and volunteer musicians. Through this position, I was provided with keyboard experience within the Lutheran Liturgical tradition in which I was raised.

• **Tenor Soloist, Substitute Organist and Music Director:** *Canton Presbyterian Church, Canton, MA* (1991-1994); I assisted in musical selection and preparation of professional (paid) quartet in which I sang tenor. At various times throughout my tenure, I was called upon to substitute for the director both as organist and conducting from the console.

Choral Experience:

• Milwukee Symphony Chorus, Boston University Choir, Boston University Singers (An eight voice ensemble; also assistant director)*, The Longy Chamber Singers*, Boston University Opera Chorus*, Grace Lutheran Choir*, Canton Presbyterian Choir*, Wisconson Honors Chorus.
* also as soloist

Education

• Post-graduate studies at Boston University in Music History with Organ emphasis-one year
• B.A. English, Music Performance minor; Boston University, 1994
• Organ studies with Jared Peck and Donna Sherwood Peck
• Conducting with Daniel Gould and Lenette Ivey

references furnished upon request

Marcus Babbitt
Pianist   AFM

145 E. 57th Street
New York, NY 10018
(212) 555-9723
(Voice Mail)

Concert Engagements

The Riverside Church (NYC)
The Rutgers Church (NYC)
Historical New York Tour
(Various locations)
SUNY at Binghamton Alumni Series (NY)
New York Athletic Club Series (NYC)
 "'A Chorus Line" (NYC)

Chamber Music Engagements

Manhattan Chamber Orchestra
• Artistic Director 1993-present
• Concerts at schools and libraries
   throughout NYC and Long Island
   Tanglewood Festival Orchestra
• Phillipe Bryere, Lance Matheson,
   Jeremy Dietz, Ribiero Gonzales,
   conductors
Babbitt Piano Trio
• Tours of East Coast and Middle East
Waverly Music Series (NYC)
Binghamton Arts League (NY)
Manhattan School Contemporary Ensemble
Brooklyn Museum (NY)

References

Credential file available:

Commercial Engagements

"Forever Plaid"
• Conductor/Pianist 1992-94
• Music Director 1994-95
• Chicago and Boston tours
"The Gondoliers" (NYC)
"West Side Story" (NYC)

Education

Manhattan School of Music
 • **Master of Music, 1993**
SUNY at Binghamton, 1988
 • **Bachelor of Fine Arts, 1991**

Principal Teachers

Piano	Master Classes
Everett Harding	Jeremy Dietz
Joshua Barr	Alan Loeber
Loren Biggs	Timothy Kelly

Radio
WCLR, Binghamton

Manhattan School of Music
Office of Placement Services
120 Claremont Avenue
New York, NY 10027

Marcus Babbitt
Pianist   **AFM**

145 E. 57th Street
New York, NY 10018
(212) 555-9723

Teaching Positions

"ArtsInfluence" NYC Public Schools
• Music program for grades 4 through 8
• Basic keyboard skills, music theory and
  ear training techniques.
• Funded by NYC Board of Education
Manhattan School Extension Program
• Workshops, seminars, performance
  opportunities for children ages 8 to 18
• Funded by Manhattan School of Music
  and New York Endowment for the Arts
Performing Arts School, NYC
Private Studio, NYC 1987-present

Arts Administration

Manhattan School of Music, 1992-93
• Masters Internship
  Office of Career Counseling

Education

  Manhattan School of Music
   • **Master of Music, 1993**
SUNY at Binghamton, 1988
   • **Bachelor of Fine Arts, 1991**

Principal Teachers

Piano   Master Classes
Everett Harding   Jeremy Dietz
Joshua Barr   Alan Loeber

References

Credential file available:

Concert Engagements

The Riverside Church (NYC)
The Rutgers Church (NYC)
Historical New York Tour
(Various locations)
SUNY at Binghamton Alumni Series
New York Athletic Club Series (NYC)

Chamber Music Engagements

Manhattan Chamber Orchestra
• Artistic Director 1993-present
• Concerts at schools and libraries
  throughout NYC and Long Island
Tanglewood Festival Orchestra
• Phillipe Bryere, Lance Matheson,
  Jeremy Dietz, Ribiero Gonzales,
  conductors
Babbitt Piano Trio
• Tours of East Coast and Middle East
Binghamton Arts League (NY)
Brooklyn Museum (NY)
Waverly Music Series (NYC)

Commercial Engagements

"Forever Plaid"
• Conductor/Pianist 1992-94
• Music Director 1994-95
• Chicago and Boston tours
"The Gondoliers" (NYC)
"West Side Story" (NYC)

Manhattan School of Music
Office of Placement Services
120 Claremont Avenue

LESTER LYONS
TENOR

456 Chicago Ave.
Chicago, IL 60613
(312) 555-2277

Height: 5' 6"
Weight: 150
Hair/Eyes: Brown

OPERA ROLES

Nemorino	*L'Elisir D'Amor*	Northeastern Il Opera
Gastone	*La Traviata*	Northeastern Il Opera
Don Ottavio	*Don Giovanni*	Northeastern Il Opera
Tamino	*DIe Zauberflote*	Northeastern Il Opera
Nankipoo	*The Mikado*	Lisle Summer Theater
Detleffe	*The Student Prince*	Lisle Summer Theater

ROLES STUDIED

Don Ottavio	*Don Giovanni*	Northeastern Illinois
Postcard form Morrocco	*Tenor*	Northeastern Illinois
Le Pecheurs de Perles	*Nadir*	Northeastern Illinois
Falstaff	*Fenton*	Northeastern Illinois

ORATORIO/CONCERT

Soloist	*Messiah*	Northeastern Symphony
Soloist	*Ninth Symphony*	Chicago Civic Orchestra
Soloist	*A Night of Mozart*	Elgin Art League

TEACHERS

Loren Jennings (current), James Steubin, Penny Christian

COACHES/DIRECTORS

Eric Lieber, Jonathan Hull, Diane Mosley, Leonardo morales, Jocylin DeBeers

EDUCATION

B.M. Voice Performance: Northeastern Illinois University (Degree expected in 1997)
Grand Lake Summer Institute: Grand Lake, WI (1995)

Elizabeth Moss
Soprano

2347 N. Oak
Lake Forest, IL 60604
(847) 555-5010

OPERA PERFORMANCES

Donna Anna	*Don Giovanni*	Skylight Opera Theater
Violetta	*La Traviata*	Northeastern U. Opera
Arminda	*La Finta Giardiniera*	Northeastern U. Opera
Desdemona	*Otello*	Northeastern U. Opera
Fiordiligi	*Così fan Tutti*	Risotto Festival

CONCERT PERFORMANCES

Ein Deutsches Requiem	Brahms	Toledo Symphony
Messiah	Handel	Northwestern University
Missa Solemnis	Beethoven	Northwestern University
Mass in C Minor	Mozart	St. James Cathedral
Gloria	Vivaldi	St. James Cathedral
Messiah	Handel	South Bend Choir

FUTURE ENGAGEMENTS

Leonore	Fidelio	Skylight Opera
Ein Deutsches Requiem	Brahms	Springfield Symphony

AWARDS AND HONORS

Siobbhan M. Horowitz Grant, 1994
Pi Lambda Nu, National Music Sorority, inducted 1990

EDUCATION AND TRAINING

Master of Music in Voice Performance, Northwestern University, in progress
Bachelor of Music in Music Education, Northwestern University, 1990

Voice: Nancy Burns Mayer, Elizabeth Crenshaw, Robert Hays
Coaches: Jordan Bonnerman, Alice Keeler, Joanne Lotti, Nathan Lowe

GEOFF BERMAN
DIRECTOR

5121 Adams Street   (708) 555-2480
Oak Park, IL 60623

THEATRE

A PLACE TO STAY	Nova Productions	Sept.-Dec. 1995

1995 WINNER - CAHN AWARD FOR OUTSTANDING PRODUCTION, DIRECTION

THE GOOD DOCTOR	Nova Productions	Sept.-Dec. 1994
THE TWO LIVES OF ALICE *Co-Authored*	Lighthouse Theatre	May 1994
LOVE AND MONEY	Trend Productions	Aug.-Sept. 1992
THE WATER ENGINE *Guest Director*	University of Southern California	June 1990
WINDOWS	USC Director's Festival April 1988	
THE HARDY BOYS GO PUNK	Live Act Players/USC	Jan.-Feb. 1986
TORCH SONG (Asst. Dir.)	USC	July 1985

MUSCIAL THEATRE

JESUS CHRIST SUPERSTAR	Playhouse Productions	May 1994
HAIR	Oak Park Theatre Guild	Sept. 1993
STARLIGHT EXPRESS	Oak Park Theatre Guild	Nov.-Dec. 1993
A CHORUS LINE	USC	April 1987
SNOOPY	USC	Nov. 1985
THE PIRATES OF PENZANCE	USC Gilbert and Sullivan	March 1994

CHILDREN'S THEATRE

A CHRISTMAS CAROL *Guest Director, fundraising event*	Oak Park Theatre Guild	Dec. 1995
THE PRINCESS AND THE PEA	Kids Klub productions	June 1995
THE FURTHER ADVENTURES OF WINNIE THE POOH	abc Playhouse	August 1994

GEOFF BERMAN
ACTOR/SINGER
Eligible Performer/EMC

5121 Adams Street
Oak Park, IL 60623
(708) 555-2480

Ht: 5'9" Wt: 140
Hair: Brn.   Eyes: Grn.
Voice: Baritone

FILM/TELEVISION

COBB	Player #5	Columbia Pictures
THE WATCHTOWER	Reporter	Universal Studios
HOME ALONE 2	Store Clerk	Hughes Entertainment
MONKEY BUSINESS	Newspaper Man	Fox Entertainment
THE CUTTING ROOM FLOOR	Waiter	CinemaScope
THE ANN DAVIS STORY	Hotel Patron	Home Box Office
ONE NIGHT ONLY	Guest Artist	Chicago Cable LASTCALL
(Ind. Feature)	Tom Darcy	I Spy Productions

INDUSTRIAL FILM

JEWEL-OSCO	Crown Communications
W.W. GRAINGER	In-House
MATRIX TELECOM	In-House

COMMERCIALS

CHICAGO SUN TIMES	Don Harper Productions
BURGER KING	Franklin-Goode
DAN LEHMAN FORD (2 SPOTS)	Video/Midwest

STAGE

FIDDLER ON THE ROOF	Motel Kamzoil	Drury Lane Theatre
WAIT UNTIL DARK	Harry	Lighthouse Theatre
MERRY WIVES OF WINDSOR	Pistol	New Shakespeare Co.
THE FANTASTICKS	Mortimer	Playhouse Productions
THREEPENNY OPERA	Beggar	Playhouse Productions

RELATED EXPERIENCE

COMEDY CLUBHOUSE Performer/Writer
(Comedy Improv Troupe - clubs, college events, corporate)

TRAINING

ACTING - James Olin   SINGING / SPEECH AND DICTION - Rudolph Glick

SPECIAL SKILLS AND INTERESTS

Most dialects, Improv, Stage Combat, Director, Stage tech, Softball, Experienced driver-manual/van/cargo truck, Great with animals.

GEOFF BERMAN

708-555-2480

Eligible Performer/EMC
Voice: Baritone

Ht: 5'9"   Wt: 140
Hair: Brn.   Eyes: Grn.

THEATRE

Wait Until Dark	Harry	Lighthouse Theatre
Merry Wives Of Windsor	Pistol	New Shakespeare Co.
Comedy of Errors	Dronio of Ephesus	New Shakespeare Co.
Devil's Advocate (Midwest Prem.)	Luke	Nova Productions
Daylight Losings	Jimmy Dean	Lighthouse Theater

MUSICAL THEATRE

Fiddler On The Roof	Motel Kamzoil	Drury Lane Theatre
The Fantasticks	Mortimer	Playhouse Productions
Threepenny Opera	Beggar	Playhouse Productions
Grease	Sonny	Lakeshore Theatre
Annie	Rooster	Lakeshore Theatre

CHILDREN'S THEATRE

Sleeping Beauty	Bad Stepdad	Kids Klub Productions
Snow White And The 7 Dudes	Narly	Kids Klub Productions
Hansel & Gretel	Owen The Wise Owl	abc Playhouse
The Adventures of Pooh	Roo	abc Playhouse

FILM/TELEVISION

Cobb	Player #5	Columbia Pictures
The Watchtower	Reporter	Universal Studios
Home Alone 2	Store Clerk	Hughes Entertainment
Monkey Business	Newspaper Man	Fox Entertainment
The Cutting Room Floor	Waiter	Cinemascope
The Ann Davis Story	Hotel Patron	Home Box Office
One Night Only	Guest Artist	Chicago Cablevision

INDUSTRIAL FILM/COMMERCIALS

Jewel-Osco	Crown Communications
W.W. Grainger	In-House
Chicago Sun Times	Don Harper Productions
Burger King	Franklin-Goode

TRAINING

Private voice lessons	Rudolph Glick
Acting	James Olin

WORKSHOPS

On-Camera	Duncan Johns
Mime	USC Mime Co.

SPECIAL SKILLS AND INTERESTS

Most dialects, Improv, Stage Combat, Technical theatre, Director, Producer

VALERIE BERNINI

24 SEAGULL LANE WILMINGTON, NC 28402 (910) 555-0835

ROLES

DON PASQUALE	NORINA	UNC OPERA THEATER
DON GIOVANNI	ZERLINA	UNC OPERA THEATER
THE MARRIAGE OF FIGARO	BARBARINA	UNC OPERA THEATER
THE FANTASTICKS	LUISA	UNC THEATER
THREE PENNY OPERA	LUCY	UNC THEATER
THE GLASS MENAGERIE	LAURA	UNC LITTLE THEATER

CHORAL EXPERIENCE

OPERA	ENSEMBLE
COSI FAN TUTTE	*UNC CHORAL UNION*
THE GONDOLIERS	*UNC CHAMBER SINGERS*
RUDDIGORE	*GREENSBORO BAROQUE*
SWEENEY TODD	*BERNINI TRIO*

EDUCATION

VOICE	ACTING	DANCE
RAQUEL LANE	CARRIE BERG	LANA DERRING
DAWN HYDE-PIERCE	JON BERWYN	BARB JACKSON
SUSAN NIX	DANIEL JAMES	ARON THEOPHOLIS

UNIVERSITY OF NORTH CAROLINA AT GREENSBORO

B.A. LIBERAL ARTS

DEBORAH BENNETT
Mezzo Soprano

OPERA

RIGOLETTO	Giovana	Cleveland Opera
CARMEN	Mercedes	Reed Dinner Theater
THE BALLAD OF BABY DOE	Augusta	Ohio U. Opera
CANDIDE	Baroness (cover)	Ohio U. Players
LA TRAVIATA	Flora	Ohio U. Opera
SUOR ANGELICA	Monitor	Ohio U. Opera

CONCERT

ELIJAH	Mendelssohn	Toledo Symphony
REQUIEM	Verdi	Wooster Chorus
MAGNIFICAT	Bach	Ohio U.Collegium
MESSIAH	Handel	Reed Baroque Ensemble
NINTH SYMPHONY	Beethoven	Toledo Festival Chorus

MUSICAL THEATER

THE PHANTOM OF THE OPERA	Madame Giry	Reed Playhouse
SWEENEY TODD	Mrs. Lovett	Reed Playhouse
A LITTLE NIGHT MUSIC	Charlotte	Wooster Rep. Theater
THE MIKADO	Katisha	Toledo Savoyards

EDUCATION

B.F.A., Ohio University, 1989
Certificate in Vocal Studies, Toledo Conservatory, 1994

PENELOPE RENATO
Mezzo Soprano

970 W. Armitage
Chicago, IL 60614
(312) 555-2875

Hair: Light Brown
Eyes: Blue
Height: 5' 6"   Weight: 140

Roles Performed

La Traviata	Flora	Chicago Opera Theater
Cosi fan Tutte	Dorabella (cover)	DePaul University
La Cenerentola	Title Role	DePaul University
Le Nozze di Figaro	Cherubino	DePaul University
Werther	Charlotte	Chautauqua Opera
Hansel and Gretel	Hansel	DePaul University
The Yeomen of the Guard	Phoebe	Northwestern University

Oratorio/Concert Performances

Handel	*Israel in Egypt*	Wheaton Symphony
Mahler	*Symphony IV*	Depaul University
Bach	*Magnificat*	Depaul University
Handel	*Messiah*	Northwestern University

Voice Teachers   Raquel Gordon (present), Nicholai Moss, Lena Armstrong

Conductors   George Hill, Fiona Rossi, John Bender, James Washington Banks

Coaches   Elaine Kirsch, Edward Grant, Hugh Stein, Richard Liotta

Awards and Honors

First Place Winner, Loggia Competition, Orzo, Italy
John F. Stein Award for Musical Excellence, DePaul University
Fellowship recipient, Northwestern University Young Artist Program

Education

Master of Music, DePaul University School of Music, Chicago, IL
Bachelor of Music, DePaul University School of Music, Chicago, IL

Beatrice Young
mezzo soprano

4501 West Mill Road
Grosse Pointe, MI 48072
313/555-1234

Height: 5' 3"   Weight: 130   Hair: Blonde   Eyes: Blue

Opera

Carmen	Mercedes	Michigan Light Opera
Carmen	Mercedes	Toledo Opera
The Marriage of Figaro	Cherubino	University of Michigan
Die Fledermaus	Prince Orlofsky	Michigan Light Opera
The Magic Flute	Second Lady	University of Michigan
Dido and Aeneas	Dido	University of Michigan
Amahl and the Night Visitors	Mother	University of Michigan

Oratorio/Concert Engagements

A Night at the Opera	Detroit Symphony
Magnificat in D	Windham Symphony Chorale
Vesperae Solemnes	Windham Symphony
Messiah	University of Michigan
Messiah	Hargrove College

"Ms. Young's voice was beautiful. . .with luster throughout the range." --Detroit Press

". . .technically polished and dramatically secure. . ." --The Sentinel (Michigan)

Awards/Honors

Metropolitan Opera Auditions	Regional Finalist	Great Lakes Region (1995)
Madeline T. Jenson Opera Award	Winner	Grosse Pointe, MI (1994)
Metropolitan Opera Auditions	District Finalist	Detroit, MI (1993)

Training

M.M., University of Michigan
B.M., University of Michigan

Teachers/Coaches: Elizabeth Allen, Jonathan Long, Suzanne Ziebler, Robert Plante, James Norton

Lisa M. Long, Percussion
282 Green Street
Jamaica Plain, MA   02117
(617) 555-5633

PRIVATE TRAINING:

Jonathan Pressman, New England Conservatory of Music;
September, 1993-May, 1995.

Michael Lawrence, Berklee School of Music; June, 1995-
December, 1995.

Patricia Stone-Berry, Wellesley Philharmonic Orchestra,
1987-1993.

PERFORMANCE EXPERIENCE:

Boston Lyric Opera Orchestra; October, 1995-April, 1996.

Wellesley Symphony Orchestra; May, 1994-present.

NEC Orchestra; September, 1993-May, 1995.

NEC Contemporary Ensemble, September, 1993-May, 1995.

NEC Wind Ensemble, September, 1994-May, 1995.

AWARDS:

Pi Kappa Lambda; May, 1995.

New England Conservatory 20th Century Achievement Prize,
1995.

Doris B.Yates International Percussion Competition, East
Coast Region; 2nd place, June 1994.

New England Artists Guild Concerto Competition; 1990.

EDUCATION:

New England Conservatory of Music, M.M.; May 1995.

Wellesley College, B.A.; May 1993.

Cary T. Christian
24 Pawnee Valley Road
Brockport, NY 14420
716-555-8102

OBJECTIVE — To teach general music (K-8) or choral music (9-12) in a challenging and progressive school setting.

EDUCATION — Eastman School of Music, May 1996
Bachelor of Music in Music Education and Organ Performance
New York State 4-Year Provisional Certification: Music, K-12

TEACHING
EXPERIENCE — Mount Vernon United Methidist Church. Vernon Hills, Indiana
Assistant Children's Choir Director/Organist, 1990-92.

-Accompanied performances of Children's Choir during Sunday services.
-Assisted in choosing appropriate sacred repertoire for young voices.
-Prepared choir in director's absence.

Sunday School Teacher, 1989-90.

Rochester School District
King Elementary School
Student Teacher, Spring, 1994.

-Assisted in teaching two choral ensembles, 5th and 6th grades.
-Assisted with general music, K-6.

Roosevelt High School
Tutor, Music and Algebra, 1992-1994.

United Methodist Midwest Arts Camp, Hammond, Indiana

-Staff Accompanist and Music Leader, 1988-1991.
-Camp Counselor, 1987-1989.

RELATED
EXPERIENCE — Eastman Madrigal Chorus
Director, 1994-1996.

Cary T. Christian
Page 2 of 2

Eastman Community Chorus
Assistant Choir Director, 1995-96.

Eastman Choral Union
Student accompanist/Tenor section leader, 1993-1996.

Eastman Gilbert and Sullivan Players
Music director/conductor for various shows, 1993-1996.

KEYBOARD
EXPERIENCE

Eastman School of Music, Rochester, New York.

-Studied organ with Douglas Bing and Roger Stanford.
-Studied piano with Roger Graham.
-Studied harpsichord with Margaret Chase Lindbergh.
-Accompanied vocalists and instrumentalists in approximately
   ten recitals yearly.
-Participated in keyboard master classes with Leonard Rudolph
   and Carter Lehman.

Ten years of piano studies with Alisa Jeffries, 1982-1992.

AWARDS

Lisette Pressman Scholarship, 1995.
Excellence in musicanship and teaching ability.

Indiana State Scholastic Achievement Award, 1992.

PROFESSIONAL
AFFILIATIONS

American Choral Directors Association
American Guild of Organists
Music Educators National Conference

Cary T. Christian
24 Pawnee Valley Road
Brockport, NY 14420
716-555-8102

OBJECTIVE   To serve as organist and choirmaster in a small but enthusiastic
             urban parish.

EDUCATION   Eastman School of Music, May 1996
             Bachelor of Music in Music Education and Organ Performance

CHURCH MUSIC Riverside Lutheran Church. Riverside, New York.
EXPERIENCE   Organist/Choirmaster, 1994-1996.

             -Coordinated music for all worship services, weekly choir
                rehearsals, weddings, funerals and special events.
             -Supervised volunteer choir and four professional section
                leaders.

             Mount Vernon United Methidist Church. Vernon Hills, Indiana
             Organist, 1991-92.

             -Provided music for Sunday services and weekly rehearsals.
             -Rehearsed Children's Choir in director's absence.

ADDITIONAL   Eastman Madrigal Chorus
CHORAL   Director, 1994-1996.
EXPERIENCE
             -Chose repetoire and conducted all rehearsals for 16 member
                choral ensemble.
             -Conducted four annual concerts as part of the College Recital
                season.

             Eastman Community Chorus
             Assistant Choir Director, 1995-96.

             -Co-conducted two concerts as part of the 1995-96 season.
             -Led weekly sectional rehearsals.

             Eastman Choral Union
             Student accompanist/Tenor section leader, 1993-1996.

-Accompanied concerts on piano.
-Led weekly tenor sectional rehearsals.
-Conducted rehearsals in director's absence.

KEYBOARD EXPERIENCE

Eastman School of Music, Rochester, New York.

-Studied organ with Douglas Bing and Roger Stanford.
-Studied piano with Roger Graham.
-Studied harpsichord with Margaret Chase Lindbergh.
-Accompanied vocalists and instrumentalists in approximately ten recitals yearly.
-Participated in keyboard master classes with Leonard Rudolph and Carter Lehman.

Ten years of piano studies with Alisa Jeffries, 1982-1992.

RELATED EXPERIENCE

Eastman Gilbert and Sullivan Players
Music director/conductor for various shows, 1993-1996.

Rochester School District
Student teacher, King Elementary School, 1994.

AWARDS

Lisette Pressman Scholarship, 1995.
Excellence in musicanship and teaching ability.

Indiana State Scholastic Achievement Award, 1992.

PROFESSIONAL AFFILIATIONS

American Choral Directors Association
American Guild of Organists
Music Educators National Conference

Brigham Charles
viola

55 Fresno Drive • Santa Fe, NM 87518 • 505/555-2674

OBJECTIVE

> • To continue to perform the viola while actively pursuing a teaching career in the field of music history.

PERFORMANCE EXPERIENCE

- Santa Fe Opera
- New Mexico Symphony
- Santa Fe Philharmonic-Substitute
- Santa Fe Conservatory Orchestra-Principal
- Santa Fe Christian College String Quartet-Founder

FESTIVALS

- Spoleto Music Festival
- Nordström International Festival, Sweden
- Bloom Lake Music Festival (Bloom Lake, OR)
- Canadian-American String Quartet Program, Vancouver, BC

EDUCATION

Santa Fe Conservatory of Music: Master of Music (1994)
- Music History and Theory

Santa Fe Christian College (1991)
- Bachelor of Arts in History
Minor in Viola Performance

Teachers: James Hendricks, Pia Herada
Coaches: Lane Myer, Penny Chase, Leonard Lewin

Brigham Charles
viola
Page 2

TEACHING EXPERIENCE

      History Dept. Santa Fe Conservatory

          • **Teaching Assistant/Lecturer**

      Spring Park Public Schools (Spring Park, NM)

          • **Tutor: Social Studies, General music**

      Adams College Musical Extension Program (Santa Fe)

          • **Private Studio, viola**

NOTABLE ACHIEVEMENTS

Publications:

"Richard Strauss: Creativity in Adversity"

      • **Masters Thesis. Published in *Music History Monthly* in November, 1994**

"A History Lesson: Teaching Children the Value of Music"

      • **Lecture prepared for presentation at Music Educators of the West Conference, June, 1994. Published in Annual Report.**

      • **To be revised and reprinted in *Musical America* in 1995**

I am currently preparing a series of lectures concerning the lack of adequate music history curriculum in the secondary schools.

Barbara Hines Johnson, Harpist

435 W. 88th Street, Apt. 5
New York, NY 10025
212/555-2245 (machine)

Orchestra Engagements	New York Philharmonic, 1992-present New Jersey Philharmonic, 1990-present New Jersey Symphony Hartford Philharmonic (CT), 1986-1987 Tanglewood Festival Orchestra Westmont Orchestra (MA), 1985-1988 Woodstock Philharmonic
Opera Engagements	New York City Opera Bronx Opera Pocket Opera (NY) New York Gilbert and Sullivan Players
Muscial Theatre	She Loves Me (Broadway) Starlight Express (Broadway) Jesus Christ Superstar The King and I Bye Bye Birdie
Reviews	"She's fantastic -- a real find!" *-New York Post* " [Ms. Hines] played with great skill and musicality..." *-Boston Globe*

Education	Mannes College of Music
	    - Master of Music, 1990
	New England Conservatory
	    - Bachelor of Music, 1988
	Tufts University
	    - Bachelor of Arts with Honors, 1988

Principal Teachers	Nina Lang-Schultz (Principal, New Jersey Philharmonic) Harold Thiessen (Principal, New York City Opera) Jeanette McPhail (Principal, Boston Symphony Orchestra)

Barbara Hines Johnson, Harpist

"Virtuosity and beauty of tone were the among the talents exhibited by the young Ms. Hines in her triumphant debut recital..."
   -New York Daily News

"...a lively performance...full of pizzazz."
   -New Jersey Sentinel

" [Ms. Hines] played with great skill and musicality..."
   -Boston Globe

"Ms. Hines Johnson captivated the audience with brilliant playing and an innate sensitivity to the music"
   -Hartford Monitor

"She's fantastic -- a real find!"
   -New York Post

SHARI ENGEL
Dancer - Choreographer - Teacher
(612) 555-3340

PERFORMING CREDITS

STAGE

- Soloist and Senior Member of JazzHot Inc., a National Touring Company. Artistic Directors : Lucie and Tag Hawkins
- Freddy Fargo's WORLD OF JAZZ DANCE 1996 - Chicago
- JADE Review '95
- JADE Review '94

MOVIES

- *The Red Shoes* Director: Donna Pescow. Choreographer: Judith Jamison, Touchstone Pictures.
- *All That Glitters* (Made for Cable) Director: Matt Spielberg, Cinemax Studios.
- *Fame* Director: Alan Parker, Paramount Pictures.
- *Never Give Up*: The Josie Johnson Story (Made for TV) Director: David Rosen.

CHOREOGRAPHY

- The Spring Dance (annual dance concert - 3 years) - University of Santa Barbara, Santa Barbara, CA
- JADE Review '92 - Malibu, CA
- Golden Hollywood (musical review) '93 - USB

TEACHING CREDITS

- Head of jazz department at Bob Fosse School for the Performing Arts in Minneapolis, MN, as well as instructor at three other local dance academies.

- Independent Choreographer-Dance Instructor for Crane High School in Malibu, CA for three years (1991-1994).

- Dance Instructor at the highly competetive Red Hill Summer Dance Program, West Redding, CA.

- Dance-Movement Instructor and Assistant Director at Gymbunnies Children's Gym in Los Angeles, CA.

- Jazz-Movement Instructor for children at four private studios and academies in the Twin Cities.

- Dance Instructor and Choreographer for dance groups throughout Los Angeles including Fox Studios and Dance Academy of the West.

- Master classes taught throughout the United States.

TRAINING

JAZZ	BALLET
Lucie and Tag Hawkins	Juliette Mitchell
Bennett DuBonn	Steven Woo
Freddie Fargo	

Elizabeth D'Arcy

School:
11 Cherry Lane Blvd.
Peachtree, GA 30321
404-555-3392

Home:
233 Delancy Street
Philadelphia, PA 02114
515-555-1451

OBJECTIVE

A position teaching strings and/or general music at the elementary or secondary level.

EDUCATION

University of Georgia, May 1992:
B.A. Music Education with string emphasis.

EXPERIENCE

Atlanta Public Schools, Atlanta, GA:
Taught strings, band, orchestra and general music to seventh through twelfth graders; prepared students for performance.

Philadelphia Public Schools, Philadelphia, PA:
Worked as a substitute teacher specializing in general music at the middle, junior high and high school levels.

City of Philadelphia Parks District:
Taught general music and art at Summer Youth Program; prepared students for weekly talent shows.

Elizabeth D'Arcy
Page Two

EXPERIENCE
(continued)

Bright Days Kid's Center:
Assisted preschool teacher; taught music classes; lead singing;
general duties as preschool teacher.

Performance Experience: Summer music festivals, 1987-1992;
Senior recital, 1991; University String Ensemble, 1990-92.

Travel: Toured Russia with Youth Chamber Orchestra at Temple
University, summer, 1986.

Professional Affiliations: Member of the Music Education
National Conference, American String Teachers Association,
and Georgia State Music Educators Association.

References and recommendations are avaiable upon request.

Lauren de Figlio

Bassoon

24 Mill Road
New Rockport, NY 12560
(914) 555-2464

EDUCATION

Oberlin Conservatory of Music: Oberlin, Ohio
    BM in Bassoon Performance/BA in Biology
    GPA: 3.62 (A+4.00)
    Date of Graduation: May, 1995

PROFESSIONAL ORCHESTRAL EXPERIENCE

Akron Symphony Orchestra (Akron, OH): principal
Brooklyn Opera Theater Orchestra (Brooklyn, NJ): 2nd
Rockport Chamber Ballet (Rockport, NY): principal
    and 2nd

OTHER ORCHESTRAL EXPERIENCE

Oberlin Orchestra: principal and 2nd
Oberlin Wind Ensemble: 2nd
Oberlin Opera Theater Orchestra: principal
MENC East Coast Orchestra: principal and 2nd
New York All-State Orchestra: associate principal

Lauren de Figlio, Bassoon
Page 2 of 2

CHAMBER MUSICAL EXPERIENCE

Oberlin Winter Term Woodwind Quintet, Midwest Tour
Oberlin Woodwind Quintet "Zepyhr"
Oberlin Chamber Winds

AWARDS AND HONORS

Lindberg Chamber Music Competition, finalist
New York All-State Scholarship Competition
Pi Kappa Lambda

TEACHERS AND OTHER REFERENCES

Robert Jernigan, Proffessor of Bassoon,
    Oberlin Conservatory
Caline Mills, Proffessor of Orchestral Conducting,
Oberlin Conservatory
Luis Garcia-Cortes, Conductor, MENC
    East Coast Orchestra

ADDITIONAL REFERENCES available upon request

PAMELA GIUFFRE
actress/model

Height: 5'8"
Weight: 106
Hair: Blonde
Eyes: Hazel

1120 N. King Rd.
Detroit, MI 43020
(616) 555-6647

Television

Bounty
Career Barbie
EZ Waterbeds
Luvs
McDonalds
Mom's Pickles
Pringles Potato Chips

Film/Industrial

Michigan Bell
Wendy's
Bessie:A Mule (short film)

Print

House & Garden
JC Penney
Leeds Inc.
Sears

Related experience

Acting: Nonnie Owens, Theo Barnett   Improv: Zack Coen
Modeling: Lara Webb Talent
Dance: 6 years ballet/modern, 2 years tap, 2 years jazz
Training: Grosse Pointe Performing Arts Centre: 5 summers
Member: Young Artists Studio (Detroit, MI) 4 years

Joshua Lieber, Clarinetist

410 St. Botolph St. #3 Boston, MA 02116 (617) 555-9504

EDUCATION	**New England Conservatory of Music** Boston, MA Bachelor of Music anticipated, May 1990
TRAINING	**Principal Teachers** David Wrightwood Laurence Pauling **Master Classes** Mimi Cohen Sam Everding **Chamber Music Coaches** Carl Evans James Brody Helen Jarrett
PERFORMANCE EXPERIENCE	**Solo Appearance** Seattle Youth Orchestra December 1988 **Orchestral** New England Conservatory Orchestra Harvard University Orchestra Longy School Orchestra **Recitals** Senior Recital January, 1990 Boston 4-H Club February, 1990 NEC Contemporary Ensemble May, 1989

luisa katarina gerasimo
tap•jazz•modern•ballet

3105 West Monroe Ave.
Fairbanks, Ohio 53422

413/555-9436

Professional Objective

Full-time position teaching dance/movement in a primary or secondary school. Willing to relocate.

Experience

September 1995 to Present
Dance/Aerobics Instructor
Pleasant Valley Adult Education
Pleasant Valley, Ohio
> Responsibilities: Plan and teach ten class sessions per week, with 15 to 20 students per class. Demonstrate and lead exercise sequences to stretch, tone, and condition participants. Also responsible for teaching students to monitor their heart rates, estimate their body-fat percentages, and set realistic health goals.

January 1993 to September 1995
Creative Movement Specialist
Dayton Day-Care
Dayton, Ohio
> Responsibilities: Developed class plans for hour-long sessions with twenty toddlers twice a week. Taught movement, dance, and exercise as age-appropriate.

gerasimo--page 1 of 2

February 1992 to December 1992
Team Teacher
Marigold Child Development Center
Dayton, Ohio
> Responsibilities*:* Taught and team taught primary students with physical disabilities (all subject areas, including physical education). Worked with other teachers and development specialists to ensure activities and curriculum was accessible to all students, regardless of their individual disabilities.

Education

> Ohio State University
> > BA, Physical Education
> > Emphasis on physiological development in children.

> Dayton Adult Education
> > Coursework in nutrition and health in adolescent and adult populations; active participant in adult women's volleyball and basketball leagues.

Certification

> Multiple-subject teaching credential.
> Certified Jazzercise instructor.

References

> Available upon request.

Dorie Johnson
Composer

1289 Carter Road
Montgomery, AL 36112

205/555-8573

EDUCATION
   University of Alabama School of Liberal and Performing Arts
      M.M., Composition/Music Technology
      B.S., Mathematical Studies

TEACHERS
   Composition: Eileen Handy, Frederick Pincus
   Music Technology: Jackson Hauser, Roger Klein, Darnell
      Wilson, Margaret Donalson
   Piano: Jacques Brodin, Judith Goodwin
   Voice: Camila McHugh, Taran Redding-Gagné, Jay Dumanian

ADDITIONAL AREAS OF STUDY
   Music: Aural skills, conducting, chamber music, music
      history, music theory, UA Choral Union
   Liberal Arts: Women's studies, American history, standard
      curriculum for mathematics major

WORKS PERFORMED
   Piano Trio No. 2 for Cello and Electric Bass, University Hall
   "Montgomery, 1968" for Tape and String Quartet, University
      Hall
   "Stormfront" Fantasy for Wind Choir and Tape, Honors
      Recital

ADDITIONAL COMPOSITIONS (Partial List)

MIDI Mini-Concerto for Synthesizer and Orchestra
String Quartet for Electric Strings
"I Wandered Lonely as a Cloud" Cantata for Voice and
    Synthesizer
Graduation Theme for Brass Quintet and Men's Chorus
    (composed for student film short)
Piano Trio No. 1
Piano Solos Nos. 1-8

MEMBERSHIPS

American Composers Workshop
Women Composers of America

REFERENCES

Available on request.

Kristina Podowlski
Conductor/Coach

82 Sidell Avenue, 5D
Long Island City, NY 11102
(718) 555-4512

CONDUCTOR

Opera/Musical Theater
Bel Canto Opera Theatre (NYC), Founder
Brooklyn Opera Theater, Conductor
Village Opera Theatre, Music Director
New York Gilbert & Sullivan Co., Music Director
Opera New York, Assistant Music Director
Trenton Opera (NJ), Cover Conductor

Orchestra
Bronx Chamber Players, Assistant Conductor
Boro Chamber Orchestra, Guest Conductor
Wildwood Music Festival, Student Orchestra

**COACH/
ACCOMPANIST**

Opera/Musical Theater
Opera Works Manhattan
Civic Theater (Kalamazoo, MI)
Wildwood Chamber Opera (NY)

Choral
Second Avenue Y Children's Choir (NYC)
Riverside Church Senior Choir (NYC)
Riverside Church Women's Chorale

Dance
Jamie Chung Studio (NYC)
Ann Arbor School of Ballet (MI)
University of Michigan Dance Classes
(Ballet, Jazz, Modern)

ORCHESTRA
(Viola)

Ann Arbor Chamber Players
Kalamazoo Civic Orchestra
University of Michigan Symphony Orchestra
University of Michigan Opera Orchestra

EDUCATION

Manhattan School of Music, M.M, 1989
University of Michigan, B.Mus., 1986

Page 1 of 2

Kristina Podowlski
Conductor/Coach

CONDUCTING SEMINARS	The Conductors Studio (NYC) Arthur Fiedler Festival at Weston (MA) Wildwood Music Festival

REPERTOIRE

OPERA	**MUSICAL/OPERETTA**	**ORCHESTRA**
Bizet *Carmen*	Bernstein *West Side Story*	Adams *Harmonium*
Britten *Peter Grimes*	Gilbert and Sullivan *HMS Pinafore* *The Gondoliers*	Bach *Brandenburg Concerto No. 2* *Magnificat*
Donizetti *Don Pasquale* *The Elixer of Love*	*Iolanthe* *The Mikado* *Pirates of Penzance*	Barber *Adagio for Strings*
Gounod *Romeo et Juliette*	Loesser *Guys and Dolls*	Beethoven *Ninth Symphony*
Menotti *The Consul* *The Medium*	Schmidt *The Fantasticks*	Brahms *Symphonies No. 3, 4*
Mozart *Cosi fan Tutte* *Don Giovanni* *Magic Flute* *Marriage of Figaro*		Copeland *Appalachian Spring* Faure *Requiem*
Offenbach *Tales of Hoffman*		Mozart *Clarinet Concerto* *Eine Kleine Nachtmusik* *Overture to Cosi fan Tutte* *Overture to Don Giovanni* *Overture to Magic Flute* *Overture to Marriage of Figaro*
Puccini *La Boheme* *Madama Butterfly*		
Strauss *Die Fledermaus*		Schubert *Unfinished Symphony*
Verdi *Falstaff* *La Traviata*		Stravinsky *L'Histoire du Soldat*

Kristina Podowlski
Conductor/Coach

"Kristina Podowlski deserves many accolades for her accompaniment and conducting of the challenging and dramatic score," said *Musician's Monthly* about her musical direction of Britten's *Peter Grimes*. Ms. Podowlski is currently Music Director of the Bel Canto Opera Theatre in New York City, which she also founded in 1993. She has conducted over 20 operatic and musical productions throughout the country. She has served on the musical staff of over 10 opera and musical theater companies and has held visiting artist positions with world renowned orchestras and choral groups.

Her extensive repertory includes such standard operatic works as *Carmen, The Marriage of Figaro, Madama Butterfly* and *La Traviata,* lesser known works such as Menotti's *The Consul,* rarely performed works such as Gounod's *Romeo et Juliette,* and much of the standard orchestral literature. Her musical and operetta credits include Bernstein's *West Side Story,* Schmidt's *The Fantasticks,* and many works by Gilbert and Sullivan.

A native of Kalamazoo, Michigan, Ms. Podowlski holds a Bachelor of Music degree form the University of Michigan, a Master of Music degree from the Manhattan School of Music and has participated in musical festivals nationwide including a recent fellowship grant to the Arthur Fiedler Festival in Weston, Massachusetts.

Natalie Coleman-Barnes
Soprano

4721 6th Avenue #3
Brooklyn, NY 11215
(718) 555-9201

Opera

Anne Trulove	The Rake's Progress
Countess	The Marriage of Figaro
Helena	A Midsummer Night's Dream
Liu	Turandot
Fiordiligi	Cosi fan Tutte
Amelia	A Masked Ball

Concert

Orff	Carmina Burana
Mozart	Mass in C Minor
Mahler	Symphony No. 4
Beethoven	Ninth Symphony

Education/Awards

San Francisco Conservatory of Music
Julliard School of Music
Tulsa Opera Center for Young Artists
Liederkrantz Award Winner
Arlene Auger Foundation Winner
AGMA Member

"Natalie Coleman-Barnes lit up the stage with effortless singing and a commanding presence" -- Marc Leighton - *Opera Review*

Francis Luis Carbajal
1415 N. Gable Lane #3
Santa Fe, NM 09005

Career Objective:

To utilize my talent as a versatile and energetic
professional dancer with experience in ballet, modern
and jazz dance.

Education:

B.F.A. - 1991
University of Orgeon, Eugene, Oregon.

Experience:

1993-1995   Performed with the Santa Fe Ballet, Under the
direction of Jan Biltmore and Roy Haggen.

Performed with Ballet Concertante under the direction
of William Forester. Santa Fe, New Mexico.

Performed as a guest soloist with Portland City Ballet,
Portland, OR.

Performed as a guest soloist with San Antonio Dance
Theater, under the direction of Nanetta DeSoto.

1992-1993   Toured Internationally as a member of Houston Ballet
under the direction of Carl Henrieksen.

1991   Performed with the Oregon Jazz Dance Factory under
the direction of Martha Hough.

1987-1990   Member of New Mexico Metropolitan Company.
Studied with Prima Ballerina Ina Esteves of El Studio
de Danza Moderna, Mexico City.

Choreography:

1994-1995	Danza Santa Fe
1992-1994	Different Drummer Rhythm Dances
1992-1993	Changing Seasons Changing
1987-1992	Choreographed for Univesity of Oregon

Teaching:

Master Classes at Santa Fe Conservatory of Dance.

Master Classes for Oregon Jazz Dance Factory.

Danza   Instructed ballet and modern classes at El Studio de Moderna, Mexico City.

Stage Movement consultant at Santa Fe Opera.

Danza   Experience with teaching children at El Studio de Moderna and Portland City Ballet.

MICHAEL SUTHERLAND

2757 Dolphin Dr. • Arnold, MD 21012 • (301)555-5390

Education   **UCLA School of Theater, Film, and TV**, Fall 1994 to present
- Comprehensive Major: Directing and Theater Management

Arnold High School, September 1990 to June 1994
- Forensics Competitive Speech Team (4 yrs.)
- Drama and Musical Productions (3 yrs.)

Awards
- Bank of Maryland Fine Arts Award - 2nd place Region Finals Scholarship, 1994
- Veterans of Foreign Wars Speech Award, 1993 and 1994
- Student of the Year - Arnold High School, 1993
- State Forensics for Thematic Interpretation - 21st place (Pieces included: Torch Song Trilogy, Into the Woods, Brighton Beach Memoirs, and Measure for Measure), 1993
- Rotary Speech Award, 1991 and 1992
- Walter Johnson Musical Comedy Award at Anne Arundel Community Stage, 1991

Performance Theater Experience

- Director, Collaborator, and Performer AIDS Teen Theater, 1994
- "Billy Crocker" in Anything Goes, 1993
- "Vincentio" in Taming of the Shrew, 1993
- "Albert" in Bye Bye Birdie, 1992
- "Frank Butler" in Annie Get Your Gun, 1991
- "Charlie" in Charlie and the Chocolate Factory, 1991
- "Ed" in You Can't Take it With You, 1991
- Writer and Performer AIDS Teen Theater, 1990 and 1991

Technical and Managing Theater Experience

Anne Arundel Community Stage
- Production Assistant - Fiddler on the Roof, 1993
- Assistant Stage Manager - Into the Woods, 1992
- Assistant Stage Manager - Camelot, 1991
- Chorus and Stage Hand - Evita, 1990
- Stage Hand - My Fair Lady, 1991

Peace Child
- Assistant Stage Manager, Props Assistant, 1990
- Assistant Technical Director, USA/USSR Production, 1990

References   Available upon request

MARK REYNOLDS
tenor

1212 Elm Ave.
South Bend, IN 46001
(812) 555-2278

Height: 5' 10"
Weight: 185
Birthdate: 8/1/68

OPERA ROLES

Spoletta	*Tosca*	Wildwood Festival
Gastone	*La Traviata*	Western IL Opera
Belfiore	*La Finta Giardiniera*	Western IL Opera
Detleffe	*The Student Prince*	Indiana Summer Rep.
Tamino	*Die Zauberflote*	Indiana College

SCENES PERFORMED

Don Ottavio (Act I)	*Don Giovanni*	South Shore Opera
Nadir (Duet with Zurga)	*Le Pecheurs de Perles*	Western IL Opera
Fenton (Act II, Sc. 2)	*Falstaff*	Western IL Opera

ORATORIO/CONCERT

Soloist: *Messiah*	Orchestra Indiana
Soloist: *Beethoven's Ninth Symphony*	Bloomington Symphony
Soloist: *Mozart Requiem*	St. John's Church, Chicago
Soloist: *Basically Bach*	Illinois Arts League

TEACHERS/CONDUCTORS/COACHES

Elizabeth Randall (present), Martin Long, Jerry Appleton, Lois Whey,
Leonard Baum, Joseph Stewart, Elaine McEnroe, Lottie Harris

OPERA TRAINING/DIRECTORS

Stephen Ross, Dolores Dunne, James Magee, Stuart Lapin

EDUCATION

M.M. Vocal Performance: Western Illinois University, 1990
B.M. Music Education: Indiana Musical College, 1987

LIZA GOLDMAN

Height: 5'9"
Weight: 145
Hair: Auburn
Eyes: Green

1456 W. Addison
Chicago, IL 60613
(312) 555-9290

VOICE OVER

America Online
Ameritech
Century 21
Chicago Cable Company
Dan DeSesto Oldsmobile
EZ-Rest Mattress & Bedding
General Nutrition Centers

New England Telephone
New Jersey Bagel Co.
Peppers Waterbeds
Ravenswood St. John's Hospital
Schaumburg Cadillac
Speedy Printers
Today's Woman

INDUSTRIAL

Burger King
Chicago Cable Company

In-house
GBH Productions

COMMERCIAL

Walgreens
CashStation
Home Depot

Roundup Productions
L.B. Jameson & Co.
Mira/Weiss Films

THEATRE

As You Like It	Audrey	Goodman Theatre
Mother Courage and Her Children	Ensemble	Halsted Theatre Centre
A Midsummer Night's Dream	Moth	Chicago Shakespeare Co.
The Merry Wives of Windsor	Mrs. Page	Chicago Shakespeare Co.
Sad Dreams, Mad Dreams (Premier)	Miss Star Cross	Moondog Theatre

TRAINING

B.A. in Theatre   Northwestern University, Chicago, Illinois
Acting: Nora Goldman, Harold Leeds, Florence Kahn, James
O'Malley
On Camera: John Burns, Leo Watson, Terry Jonas
Dance: Includes 4 years ballet, 2 years modern, 3 years jazz and tap

SPECIAL SKILLS

Fluent in Spanish; Conversational Italian; Dilects: Standard British, American
Southern, New England American; Irish brogue; Gymnastics, Softball, Aerobics

LIZA GOLDMAN

Height: 5'9"
Weight: 145
Hair: Auburn
Eyes: Green

1456 W. Addison
Chicago, IL 60613
(312) 555-9290

THEATRE

Hearts Adrift	Annabelle	Touchstone Theatre
Margot and the Monkey	Margot	Skylit Repertory
As You Like It	Audrey	Goodman Theatre
	Phebe	Civic Theater
Magic Acts	Fawn	Skylit Repertory
Mother Courage and Her Children	Ensemble	Halsted Theatre *101*
Dalmations	Miss Pongo	Pipeline Theatre
Cloud 9	Betty/Edward	New Theater
A Midsummer Night's Dream	Moth	City Shakespeare
Come Back to the 5 & Dime...	Sissy	Crossroads
The Merry Wives of Windsor	Mrs. Page	City Shakespeare
Sad Dreams, Mad Dreams (Premier)	Miss Star Cross	Moondog Theatre
Rites	Theresa (u.s.)	Halsted Theatre

TRAINING

B.A. in Theatre	Northwestern University, Chicago, Illinois
Acting:	Nora Goldman, Harold Leeds, Florence Kahn
On Camera:	John Burns, Leo Watson, Terry Jonas
Movement:	Carol Render, Rich Hull, Suzy Lee, Manny Pierson
Dance:	Includes 4 years ballet, 2 years modern, 3 years jazz, 2 years Tap, Feldenkreis Method
Acting Apprentice:	Newton Theatre Festival

SPECIAL SKILLS

Fluent in Spanish; Conversational Italian; Dilects: Standard British,Southern and New England American; Irish brogue; Gymnastics, Softball, Jogging, Aerobics, Rollerblading, Painting

GABRIELA PETERS
Soprano

240 W. 53rd St., #5B
New York, NY 10001
(212) 555-2274

OPERA

Le Nozze di Figaro	Cherubino
The Turn of the Screw	Governess
Don Pasquale	Norina
Il Barbiere di Siviglia	Rosina

ROLES STUDIED

Rigoletto	Gilda
Cosi fan Tutte	Dorabella
Ariande auf Naxos	Zerbinetta
L'Egisto	Amor

TRAINING

Boston Conservatory of Music, B.M., 1995
    Voice: Elaine Grissell, David Corson
    Master Classes: Mari Martin, Jan DeGreux, Robert Capon

AWARDS/FESTIVALS

Finalist. Regional Metropolital Opera Auditions, 1994
Tanglewood Music Festival, 1995
Aspen Music Festival, 1994

KEVIN JOHNSON
Tenor

Home Address:
35 Seaview Lane
Westport, CT 06821
(203) 555-1987

School Address:
MCCM Mailbox # 708
St.Paul, MN 44074
(612) 555-6073

OPERA (Roles and Chorus)

The Marriage of Figaro (Don Basilio)
Dialogues of the Carmelites (First Officer)
The Rake's Progress
Cosi fan Tutte
La Traviata

SCENES STUDIED

The Magic Flute (Tamino)
The Marriage of Figaro (Don Basilio)
The Bartered Bride (Vasek)

PROFESSIONAL AND SOLO EXPERIENCE

Soloist, McCall College Musical Union
Soloist, McCall College Choir, East Coast Tour
Chorus Member and Soloist, Trinity Church, Sioux Falls, MN
Tenor Section Leader, St. James Episcopal Chuch, Norwalk, CT

HONORS

Second Place, NATS Vocal Competition, Midwest Region
Second Place, NATS Vocal Competition, Junior Division, Midwest
Music Achievement Award, Logan Senior High School, Westport, CT

MAJOR VOICE TEACHERS

Frederick Andersen (current teacher), Associate Prof. of Singing, McCall
Donetta Cole, Director, Logan Mixed Choir, Logan Senior High School

EDUCATION

McCall Conservatory of Music and McCall College
Double Major: Voice Performance and German, expected in May, 1988

MARTIN ALONZO
Tenor

525 N. Oaktree Drive
Seattle, WA 55020
704-555-6683

Hair: Black
Eyes: Brown
Height: 6'2"

OPERA / OPERETTA

El Diablo (Premiere)	OPERA ETCETERA	Daniele
Viva las Vegas! (Premiere)	KLEIN OPERA	Elvis
Der Kommissar (U.S. Prem.)	SCENA PRODUCTIONS	Heinrick
The Seer (Northwest Premiere)	MAYNOR OPERA THEATER	Lancelot
The Silent Queen	MAYNOR OPERA THEATER	Angel

MUSICAL THEATRE

The Great Waldo Pepper	PONY PRODUCTIONS	Title Role
American Werewolf	AROUND THEATER	Frank
A Little More Love	MAYNOR THEATRE GROUP	Newton
Happy Jack (Premiere)	MAYNOR THEATRE GROUP	Jack/Mars

CONCERT / RECITAL

A Night in Venezuela	SEATTLE CIVIC SYMPHONY	Soloist
Bach Canatatafest	MAYNOR COLLEGE	Soloist
Verdi Requiem	MAYNOR COLLEGE	Soloist
Adams Symphony "Homer"	WASHINGTON ARTS CENTRE	Soloist
Mozart C Minor Mass	ST. CEPHUS CHURCH	Soloist

EDUCATION /STUDIES

Opera Workshops	AMERICAN COLLEGE OF MUSIC	A. Waldman
Opera Workshops	SHERWOOD CONSERVATORY	S. Simonson
Private Voice	MAYNOR COLLEGE OF THE ARTS	L. Hodge
Vocal Coaching	MAYNOR COLLEGE OF THE ARTS	D. Nedda

SPECIAL SKILLS / INTERESTS

Languages: Fluent in Spanish, Italian and English; Various voices and dialects
Other Interests: Photography, Songwriting, Weightlifting, Golf

Chapter Six

SAMPLE COVER LETTERS

Kenneth M. Shannon
flute

February 1, 19--

Don Sullivan, Director
Richmond Summer Institute
545 N. Seaview
Richmond, VA 22031

Dear Mr. Sullivan:

Please accept my resume as a precursor to the application process for the Summer Institute.

I am currently studying flute performance at the Boulder School of Music, University of Colorado. I feel that your intensive program that combines orchestral performance with chamber and repertory classes is exactly what I need to continue my education during my summer break. I will be applying for a scholarship if accepted to audition, but am aware that this has no bearing on your decision.

As a native of Virginia, I am very excited at the prospect of working with you at the institute.

Thank you very much for your time. I look forward to hearing from you soon.

With regards,

Kenneth M. Shannon

School Address:	Summer Address:
Marks Hall, Room 224	45 Long Avenue
Boulder, CO 80310	Arlington, VA 22202
(303) 555-3120	(703) 555-3574

JACOB LANG
BASS

245 N. ABBOTT DRIVE
BLOOMINGTON, IN 46802
812-555-6144

SEPTEMBER 10, 19--

BEL CANTO FOUNDATION
P.O. BOX 652
WILMETTE, IL 60625

DEAR COMPETITION COORDINATOR:

I AM A BASS PURSUING MY DEGREE IN PERFORMANCE AT INDIANA UNIVERSITY. I AM INTERESTED IN AUDITIONING TO COMPETE IN THE JUNIOR DIVISION (AGES 18 - 22) OF YOUR UPCOMING COMPETITION. I UNDERSTAND THAT I WILL BE COMPETING IN THE MIDWEST REGION IF MY APPLICATION IS ACCEPTED.

PLEASE SEND ME AN APPLICATION AND ANY OTHER MATERIALS NECESSARY TO COMPLETE THIS PROCESS. I HAVE ENCLOSED MY RESUME IN ADVANCE FOR YOUR INFORMATION AND CONSIDERATION.

I LOOK FORWARD TO HEARING FROM YOU SOON.

SINCERELY,

JACOB LANG

Beatrice Young
mezzo soprano

4501 W. Mill Road
Grosse Pointe, MI 48072
(313) 555-8019

May, 19--

Greater Michigan Opera Theater
8922 Three Pines Road
Lansing, Michigan 44026

To Whom It May Concern:

I am a mezzo soprano with a master's degree in voice from the University of Michigan. I am seeking opprtunities in young artist programs and am greatly interested in your company. As a resident of Michigan, I am very familiar with the Opera Theater and would love the opprtunity to work with you in future seasons.

This season I was a finalist in the Metropolitan Opera Auditions, Great Lakes District. Recent solo highlights include performances with the Detroit Symphony and the Windham Chorale. My diverse operatic repertoire includes Mercedes in *Carmen*, The Second Lady in *The Magic Flute*, and Mother in *Amahl and the Night Visitors*.

Please send me any information you have regarding the Young Artist Opera Theater Program. I am available to audition at any time. I greatly look forward to hearing from you.

Sincerely,

Beatrice Young

STEPHANIE T. CORMAN

Double Bass

114 E. 23rd Street #16B
New York, NY 10018
212-555-0213

November 15, 19--

Eugene Bibbs
Personnel Director
San Diego Philharmonic
San Diego, CA 93188

Dear Mr. Bibbs:

I would like to audition for the position of assistant principal double bass with the San Diego Philharmonic Orchestra. My performance degree is from the Juilliard School of Music where I study with Vaughan Chambers. I will receive the degree in May at which time I will return to the West Coast.

My performance experience includes the following:

San Francisco Symphony Orchestra	1995
Greenwich Symphony Orchestra: principal	1994-present
Mt. Vernon Chamber Players	1992-1994
Juilliard Chamber Orchestra: principal	1995-present
Juilliard Contemporary Ensemble: assistant principal	1993-present
Juilliard Orchestra: assistant principal	1992-present

Earlier this year I was one of three finalists for the principal double bass position with the Dayton Symphony. I am a former student of Robert Pytorski, principal with the San Francisco Symphony, and continue to have lessons with him whenever I am in the Bay Area.

Please send me your audition schedule and a list of repertoire for the season. Thank you for your consideration.

Sincerely,

Stephanie Corman

June 15, 19--

Dr. Ariel Blumfield
Admissions Director
New England College of Music
330 Columbus Avenue
Boston, MA 02115

Dear Dr. Blumfield:

I am a recent college graduate with a bachelor's degree in French horn performance from the Peabody Conservatory of Music. Having recently returned to the New England area, I am greatly interested in your school. As indicated by my resume, I have extensive performance experience and am a member of several musical organizations.

I am currently studying with Donna Burke, and as she is on your adjunct faculty for the upcoming year, I would continue to study with her were I accepted into the program.

Please send me any information you may have regarding your graduate performance program. I would expect to matriculate with the class of 1998 given a standard two-year program.

Please also feel free to contact Ms. Burke at (207) 555-7878 for further reference.

Thank you very much for your time. I look forward to hearing from you.

Sincerely,

Michael Alan Pierce
145 Main Street #2
Bangor, ME 04322
(207) 555-3236

Martha Garrett, Oboe
68447 Owahu Drive
Honolulu, Hawaii 96732
808-555-4700

April 30, 19--

Audition Committee
Cleveland Orchestra
P.O. Box 2657
Cleveland, OH 44025

Dear Sirs:

I am interested in the position of Principal Oboe. As a player with experience in orchestras throughout the country, I feel I would be an asset to the section. I have enclosed my résumé for your consideration. I would be happy to provide any references you might require for invitation to audition.

Thank you for your time. I look forward to hearing from you.

Sincerely,

Martha Garrett

Cary T. Christian
24 Pawnee Valley Road
Brockport, NY 14420
716-555-8102

March 30, 19--

Dr. Alan Hessman
Jefferson Public Academy
111 N. Dobson Blvd.
White Plains, New York 12461

Dear Dr. Hessman,

I thoroughly enjoyed our telephone conversation on Friday, March 26th, and am following up with the résumé you requested. As you may remember, I am anticipating graduation in May with my B.A. in Education and Performance from Eastman School of Music and am seeking a teaching position in your middle school. With ten years of experience teaching at the elementary, high school, and university level, I feel prepared to enter the public school sector as a skilled and qualified teacher.

The enclosed resume highlights my teaching experience and conducting positions at the School of Music. In addition to these duties, I was deeply involved in the Rochester School District. I feel strongly that music plays an integral part in a child's development. I believe I can promote an understanding and love of music that is sorely needed in the public school system.

I both acknowledge and commend you and your school on such fine work in this and many other areas to date. I would like to become a part of such essential work in the future.

I look forward to hearing from you.

Sincerely,

Cary Thomas Christian

Sarah J. Lindenbaum

Home Address:
152 North Avenue
Wilmette, IL 60122
(847) 555-3388

School Address:
33 Maple Ave.
Ann Arbor, MI 49023
(413) 555-6672

May 1, 19--

Beatrice Russell, Principal
Andrews Academy
Freeport, Connecticut 05845

Dear Ms. Russell,

As a 1989 graduate with a Bachelor of Music Education from the University of Michigan School of Music, I am interested in being a member of the faculty of Andrews Academy.

I am attracted to Andrews Academy because of its strong commitment to giving a high quality education to "high risk" children. The progressive and innovative philosophy of encouraging such students to reach their full potential through musical expression proves the school's dedication to the arts.

The enclosed resume highlights both my performance experience and teaching credentials. My experiences as a lecturer have included historical performance classes with special emphasis on The Renaissance Period. I have taught cello in the Ann Arbor Public School System as well as at the university level. In addition to teaching, I have coached chamber music at all levels of ability. My extracurricular interest and skills in singing and dance will also be an asset to becoming a successful teacher. I have the needed energy, cooperative spirit, dedication and skills to make a positive contribution to your school.

Although I am not currently enrolled in school, I am prepared to enter a master's program in conjunction with the position, if this is desired. Please let me know how to proceed. I will be returning to the East Coast in July, but will be available to interview by telephone until that time.

Thank you so much for your time and consideration.

Sincerely,

Sarah Lindenbaum

Elizabeth Moss
Soprano

2347 N. Oak
Lake Forest, IL 60605
(847) 555-5010

September 1, 19--

Toledo Opera Theater
P.O. Box 39270
Toledo, OH 44023

Dear Toledo Opera Theater:

Please accept the enclosed résumé and photo for your files. I am seeking opportunities as a principal or chorus member and would appreciate receiving your audition schedule or any information you have in that regard.

I look forward to hearing from you.

Sincerely,

Elizabeth Moss

enclosures: résumé/photo

MARTIN ALONZO
Tenor

525 N. Oaktree Drive
Seattle, WA 55020
704-555-6683

Fall, 19--

To Whom it May Concern:

I am sending the enclosed resume for your consideration. As illustrated by my resume, I am a versatile and energetic performer with extensive experience in opera, operetta, concert, and theatre, specializing in original works. I am seeking to further expand my portfolio and would appreciate any information you may have regarding auditions with your company.

Thank you for your time and effort. I look forward to hearing from you.

Sincerely,

Martin Alonzo

RONALD A. SANDLER
22 Ridge Avenue
Lexington, MA 02113
(617) 555-3212

September 15, 19--

Mrs. Najera Roe
Auditions Committee Coordinator
Boston Symphony Orchestra
One Massachusetts Avenue
Boston, MA 02115

Dear Mrs. Roe:

I am a recent graduate of New England Conservatory with a master's degree with honors in performance, and I am interested in taking your upcoming audition for substitute principal trumpet. I am currently studying with Rudolph Blintz and am sending my résumé upon his recommendation. I am aware that the audition process is very selective, but I trust that you will give my credentials fair consideration. Needless to say, it would be an honor to play for your committee.

If you have any questions or require further recommendations, please contact me at your convenience. I greatly look forward to hearing from you.

Sincerely,

Ronald A. Sandler

enclosure: résumé

Barry Kim
16 Brookfield Road • Hartford, CT O7450 • 203/555-7879

March 22, 19--

Mrs. Jeannie Hartmann, Director
Rosewood Summer Theater
10 *The Woodlands*
Rosewood, VT 05660

Dear Mrs. Hartmann:

I am a junior at the Ethel Barrymore High School for the Performing Arts in LaFayette, New York. I am writing to obtain information regarding your theater company and am interested primarily in performance opportunities.

Although I have never been employed by a theater company, I have attended the Hartt Performance Center for Young Artists for five consecutive summers in addition to adhering to the rigorous schedule and curriculum of the High School for the Performing Arts during the school year.

As my resume indicates, I have had training in acting, singing, dance, and stage combat as well as piano. My recent performance credits include the title role in the *King and I* at the high school and an appearance as a soloist in Bernstein's *Chichester Psalms* at Mount Sinai Temple in LaFayette, for which I received a favorable mention in the *LaFayette Gazette*.

I believe a position with your company would be excellent preparation for a performing arts career. Thank you in advance for your time.

Yours sincerely,

Barry Kim

Beverly Whitfield

61 Sanders Ave. #302
New Haven, CT 07450
(203) 555-1644

April 1, 19--

Newcastle Summer Theater
P.O. Box 250
Newcastle, Maine 04030

Dear Newcastle Summer Theater:

I am writing to inquire about your theater program. I am an actress and a student with a degree in English with an emphasis in theater. As indicated by the enclosed resume, however, my extracurricular stage experience is extensive and greatly served to enhance my academic endeavors.

Although I am primarily seeking to expand my acting portfolio, I am interested in your technical program as well.

Please send me any information you have in regard to both programs, or contact me at the above number. Thank you very much.

I look forward to hearing from you soon.

Cordially,

Beverly Whitfield

June 10, 19--

Elia M. Gray
C/O Capri Artists Ltd.
130 W. 10th Street
Suite 302
New York, NY 10012
(212) 555-5434

Lana Barnes Mitchell, Casting
The Elaine Stevens Show
25 Rockefeller Plaza Suite 1010
New York, NY 10122

Dear Ms. Mitchell,

I am writing to you as a working actress and stand-up comedienne who would like very much to be considered for work on "The Elaine Stevens Show." Under fives and extra work would always be a wonderful addition to my expanding resume. I also think it's the best show out there by far. I tape it every day! I recently finished writing a one-woman show which I hope to produce this fall.

Thank you for your time and consideration. I look forward to having the opportunity to audition for you soon.

Sincerely,

Elia M. Gray

Michael Dodge
18 Crestwell Lane
Dubuque, IA 52008
312-555-0980

June 10, 19--

Ms. Patricia Dobson-Hull
Assistant Director of Marketing
Iowa State Opera
One Grace Plaza
Ames, IA 53221

Dear Ms. Dobson-Hull:

I am writing to follow up on our conversation of June 5th. As you may recall, I am a graduate of Grinnell College interested in the position of public relations assistant in your marketing department.

As we discussed, I am enclosing my resume for your consideration. I believe that a small but growing company such as yours would be the perfect place for me to build upon my skills in the field of arts management. My varied work experience as an admissions assistant at Grinnell, in addition to work with the Iowa Symphony and extracurricular performance activities, should further indicate my suitability for the position.

Please contact me at the above address in the event of an interview. I greatly enjoyed talking to you and look forward to hearing from you again soon.

Sincerely,

Michael Dodge

Michael Dodge
18 Crestwell Lane
Dubuque, IA 52008
312-555-0980

July 15, 19--

Mr. Jim Lee, GC '81
2828 N. Pine Grove
Chicago, IL 60657

Dear Mr. Lee:

I am a recent graduate of Grinnell College with a bachelor's degree in music, looking for a position in arts management. Jan Vitner, a career placement counselor at Grinnell, thought that you might be a good lead to any possibilities in the field in the Chicago area. I will be moving there in September and hope to secure employment by that time.

I have enclosed a resume for your inspection. If you know of anyone who is in need of talents like mine in the near future, please let me know, or call their attention to my resume. Any assistance you can offer in this regard would be greatly appreciated.

In any event, I am interested in any suggestions you may have for a recent graduate with performance and management skills going out into the "real world." Please let me know if I may call you when I am in Chicago next month. I would like to discuss these matters further in person at your convenience. I look forward to meeting you.

Sincerely,

Michael Dodge

Laralynn Jennings
234 Mapletree Avenue
Baltimore, MD 21216
410-555-5478

September 20, 19--

Mrs. Marsha Ames Wallace
Silver Spring School of Dance
10 Shady Tree Road
Silver Spring, MD 20901

Dear Mrs. Wallace,

In December 1995, I will graduate from the University of Maryland with a BFA in dance. I am seeking part-time teaching opportunities. Having received a scholarship to attend the Silver Spring School in the Summer of 1988, and remembering that experience with great fondness, I immediately thought to write and update you as to my progress.

In the past four years I have received extensive training and have gained substantial performance experience as a dancer, with most attention to ballet and modern. In additon to the required courses , I have done supplementary work in jazz and tap at the Rosario Dance Studio where I am also currently a teacher.

Additional teaching experience includes two years at Dance Baltimore where I teach ballet and jazz. For the last three years I have concurrently maintained a small private studio under the auspices of the University.

My early experiences at the Silver Spring School and the Washington School of the Arts contributed greatly to my love of dance and continue to fuel my desire to teach.

I appreciate your taking the time to review my resume. I am interested specifically in positions available at the beginning of next year. Thank you for your consideration; I look forward to meeting you.

Sincerely Yours,

Laralynn Jennings

After December 15th:
14 Monarch Drive
Takoma Park, MD 20911
(301) 555-6954

Laralynn Jennings
234 Mapletree Avenue
Baltimore, MD 21216
410-555-5478

September 20, 19--

Babette Lyons, Editor
DanceArt Magazine
1000 9th Street
Washington, DC 20015

Dear Ms. Lyons,

In December 1995, I will be a graduate of the University of Maryland with a BFA in dance. I am seeking a position in at any level in the dance field, preferably as a performer, but I am also seeking part-time teaching opprtunities. Mira Browning, my advisor and teacher, recommended that I contact you for information concerning job opportunities in the field. I am interested specifically in positions available at the beginning of next year.

In the past four years I have received extensive training and have gained substantial performance experience as a dancer, with most attention to ballet and modern. In additon to the required courses , I have done supplementary work in jazz and tap at the Rosario Dance Studio, where I also teach.

Additional teaching experience includes two years at Dance Baltimore where I teach ballet and jazz to children and adults. For the last three years I have concurrently maintained a small private studio.

I would appreciate any information concerning available positions, or names and addresses of other people whom I could contact. If it would be more convenient, I would be glad to call you. Please let me know when and where it is best to reach you.

Sincerely Yours,

Laralynn Jennings

After December 15th:
14 Monarch Drive
Takoma Park, MD 20911
(301) 555-6954

Ginny Rae Bell
comedienne

P.O. Box 2282
San Jose, CA
510 • 555 • 7382

January 22, 19--

Nicole Gerson, Casting Director
Comedy Acts Live
Comedy Central
40 Rockefeller Center
New York, NY 10122

Dear Ms. Gerson,

I am an energetic and creative comedienne who would very much like to be a part of *Comedy Acts Live*. I have been watching the show since it began and believe that my versatile talents would be a perfect fit with the show's unique brand of humor.

I am interested in either writing or performing on the show, but will accept anything that is available in order to be a part of what I believe to be the funniest half hour on television. I have been living in the San Jose area but would be happy to relocate if an offer came along that I couldn't refuse!

I am enclosing a recent headshot and resume for you to consider. Most recently, I have produced a comedy showcase at the House of Comedy in Berkeley which is scheduled to run again this spring. Please come and catch the show if you're ever in the Bay Area.

I thank you for your time and hope to have the pleasure of meeting you soon.

Sincerely,

Ginny Rae Bell

DANICA HARRIS
COLORATURA SOPRANO

508 9TH STREET • BROOKLYN, NY 11215 • (718) 555-3735

APRIL 3, 19~~

MS. SHARI ENGEL
PRESIDENT, CONCERT ARTISTS NEW YORK
220 LEXINGTON AVENUE
NEW YORK, NEW YORK 10022

DEAR MS. ENGEL:

    IT WAS A GREAT PLEASURE LISTENING TO YOUR LECTURE AND TALKING WITH YOU AT THE SINGERS' WORKSHOP AT BROOKLYN COLLEGE TODAY. I FEEL INSPIRED BY YOUR SUCCESSFUL CAREER AS AN AGENT AND BUSINESSWOMAN AND THE ENERGY AND DRIVE WHICH LED YOU TO THAT SUCEESS.

    I PLAN TO FOLLOW THE ADVICE YOU GAVE ME REGARDING MY MATERIALS WHILE CONTACTING THE PEOPLE YOU MENTIONED, AND WILL KEEP YOU INFORMED OF MY PROGRESS. I HOPE TO HAVE THE PLEASURE OF WORKING YOU WITH YOU SOME TIME IN THE FUTURE.

    THANK YOU!

    YOURS SINCERELY,

DANICA HARRIS

VGM CAREER BOOKS

BUSINESS PORTRAITS
Apple
Boeing
Coca-Cola
Ford
Kellogg's
McDonald's

CAREER DIRECTORIES
Careers Encyclopedia
Dictionary of Occupational Titles
Occupational Outlook Handbook

CAREERS FOR
Animal Lovers; Bookworms; Car Buffs;
Caring People; Computer Buffs; Crafty
People; Culture Lovers; Environmental
Types; Fashion Plates; Film Buffs; Foreign
Language Aficionados; Good Samaritans;
Gourmets; Health Nuts; History Buffs;
Kids at Heart; Music Lovers; Mystery
Buffs; Nature Lovers; Night Owls;
Number Crunchers; Plant Lovers; Self-
Starters; Shutterbugs; Sports Nuts; the
Stagestruck; Travel Buffs; Writers

CAREERS IN
Accounting; Advertising; Business; Child
Care; Communications; Computers;
Education; Engineering; the
Environment; Finance; Government;
Health Care; High Tech; Horticulture &
Botany; International Business;
Journalism; Law; Marketing; Medicine;
Science; Social & Rehabilitation Services;
Travel, Tourism, & Hospitality

CAREER PLANNING
Beating Job Burnout
Beginning Entrepreneur
Big Book of Jobs
Career Planning & Development for
   College Students & Recent Graduates
Career Change
Career Success for People with Physical
   Disabilities
Careers Checklists
College and Career Success for Students
   with Learning Disabilities
Complete Guide to Career Etiquette
Cover Letters They Don't Forget
Dr. Job's Complete Career Guide
Executive Job Search Strategies
Guide to Basic Cover Letter Writing
Guide to Basic Resume Writing
Guide to Internet Job Searching
Guide to Temporary Employment
Job Interviewing for College Students
Joyce Lain Kennedy's Career Book
Out of Uniform
Parent's Crash Course in Career Planning

Slam Dunk Cover Letters
Slam Dunk Resumes
Up Your Grades: Proven Strategies for
   Academic Success

CAREER PORTRAITS
Animals; Cars; Computers; Electronics;
Fashion; Firefighting; Food; Music;
Nature; Nursing; Science; Sports;
Teaching; Travel; Writing

GREAT JOBS FOR
Art Majors
Business Majors
Communications Majors
Engineering Majors
English Majors
Foreign Language Majors
History Majors
Liberal Arts Majors
Psychology Majors
Sociology Majors

HOW TO
Apply to American Colleges and
   Universities
Approach an Advertising Agency and Walk
   Away with the Job You Want
Be a Super Sitter
Bounce Back Quickly After
   Losing Your Job
Change Your Career
Choose the Right Career
Cómo escribir un currículum vitae en
   inglés que tenga éxito
Find Your New Career Upon Retirement
Get & Keep Your First Job
Get Hired Today
Get into the Right Business School
Get into the Right Law School
Get into the Right Medical School
Get People to Do Things Your Way
Have a Winning Job Interview
Hit the Ground Running in Your New
   Job
Hold It All Together When You've Lost
   Your Job
Improve Your Study Skills
Jumpstart a Stalled Career
Land a Better Job
Launch Your Career in TV News
Make the Right Career Moves
Market Your College Degree
Move from College into a
   Secure Job
Negotiate the Raise You Deserve
Prepare Your Curriculum Vitae
Prepare for College
Run Your Own Home Business

Succeed in Advertising When all You
   Have Is Talent
Succeed in College
Succeed in High School
Take Charge of Your Child's Early
   Education
Write a Winning Resume
Write Successful Cover Letters
Write Term Papers & Reports
Write Your College Application Essay

MADE EASY
Choosing a Career
College Applications
Cover Letters
Getting a Raise
Job Hunting
Job Interviews
Resumes

ON THE JOB: REAL PEOPLE WORKING IN...
Communications
Health Care
Sales & Marketing
Service Businesses

OPPORTUNITIES IN
This extensive series provides detailed
   information on more than 150 individual career fields.

RESUMES FOR
Advertising Careers
Architecture and Related Careers
Banking and Financial Careers
Business Management Careers
College Students &
   Recent Graduates
Communications Careers
Computer Careers
Education Careers
Engineering Careers
Environmental Careers
Ex-Military Personnel
50+ Job Hunters
First-Time Job Hunters
Government Careers
Health and Medical Careers
High School Graduates
High Tech Careers
Law Careers
Midcareer Job Changes
Nursing Careers
Performing Arts Careers
Re-Entering the Job Market
Sales and Marketing Careers
Science Careers
Scientific and Technical Careers
Social Service Careers

VGM Career Horizons
a division of *NTC/Contemporary Publishing*
4255 West Touhy Avenue
Lincolnwood, Illinois 60646–19753